MEMORIES OF
REINCARNATION

MEMORIES OF REINCARNATION

Grace Cooke

WHITE EAGLE PUBLISHING TRUST
NEW LANDS · LISS · HAMPSHIRE · ENGLAND

THE ILLUMINED ONES
first published October 1966,
itself based on PLUMED SERPENT (1942)
and THE SHINING PRESENCE (1946)
First published under this title
August 2006

British Library Cataloguing-in-Publication Data
A catalogue record for this book is available
from the British Library

ISBN 978-0-85487-174-2

Set in 10.5 on 14pt Baskerville at the Publishers
and printed in China by Artical Printing

Contents

Preface

WHEN Grace Cooke, who was my grandmother, was writing the original edition of this book, using some material from her earlier books PLUMED SERPENT and THE SHINING PRESENCE, and adding new material, I was privileged to be working with her as her secretary. I was only eighteen at the time, and although I had been brought up with spiritual teaching and knowledge of her guide, White Eagle, I had not then really experienced at first hand the extraordinary work of the illumined teachers of whom she writes, or of White Eagle himself and the spiritual Brotherhood of which he is part (the next section, entitled 'Who is White Eagle?', explains this reference). However, I did recognize something special about the stories she was relating and felt strongly the presence of her teacher, White Eagle, as she dictated passages for me to type and talked of her memories of working with White Eagle in past lives. She also discussed with me my work with her and White Eagle in those former lives, and told me that I was her sister in the life with Hah-Wah-Tah.

Grace Cooke passed to spirit in 1979 but even forty years after it was first published, I believe this is a very important book to keep in print alongside the many books that contain White Eagle's own words. His teaching is indeed a profound philosophy for life and a restatement of the ancient wisdom that has been a part of mystic and occult groups down the ages. However, it is also absolutely relevant to life in the twenty-first century. This book brings a new dimension to the teaching found in the White Eagle books, because it relates human stories of life in the physical world that illustrate the spiritual truths contained in the teaching. It also paints a convincing picture of divine guidance and inspiration spanning many lifetimes and gives an overall a vision of unfolding brotherhood and the beauty of 'the heavenly scheme of things' leading eventually to a time of greater understanding, harmony and wellbeing for all life on earth.

This book is being re-issued at the same time as a new book of White Eagle's teaching entitled White Eagle on Reincarnation is also being published. They can be read as companion volumes.

Who is White Eagle?

MANY years ago, speaking through Grace Cooke, White Eagle himself said:*

'We come to you under the name of White Eagle, but would explain that we speak for a large company of shining beings, angels and illumined souls of men and women who are sometimes referred to as 'the Star brotherhood'.

'We have the name of White Eagle because our message is the message of John, the beloved of the Lord Jesus. John is the 'light bringer'; White Eagle is the humble servant, but the symbol of the white eagle is one used by John the Beloved, the teacher of the new Age of Aquarius. This light is gradually being born upon your earth plane. Many messengers are coming to the earth from the higher spheres of life with the same message.

*This passage is quoted from the book THE LIGHT BRINGER, published by The White Eagle Publishing Trust

'It is a very simple message—the one which Jesus left with his disciples—*love one another.*

'We have worked for many incarnations in the personality we take on when we come into physical conditions, to bring to men and women an understanding of the brotherhood of all life, so that the kingdom of God shall come upon earth. But this can only happen when men and women have discovered that within their own souls is the light of the spirit of Christ, the Christ light which is the seed given to every one of them.'

The work of the illumined teacher we know as White Eagle is to help people awaken their own inner guidance, their intuition, or the light of the spirit that is within every human soul. His teachings are filled with love and understanding for the difficulties we all face. There are actually many reasons why White Eagle has chosen his particular symbolic name; for example, it signifies one with spiritual vision. The Native Americans have a legend that the name White Eagle means a spiritual teacher because 'the white eagle flies straight towards the sun'. In the Ancient Mysteries, the eagle symbolised the higher psychic and spiritual powers of human kind. It indicated one who had developed the power to penetrate with clear vision (clairvoyance) into the inner and secret worlds.

In the first edition of this book, published under the title THE ILLUMINED ONES, Grace Cooke herself wrote an introductory chapter on the subject of who she believed White Eagle to be. Here follows some of what she wrote then.

'Who is White Eagle?', people sometimes ask. He is always enigmatical about this and seems to discourage the subject. But many years ago when he first made himself known to me he said that his most recent incarnation was as a Mohawk chief of the league of the Six (formerly five) Nations of the Iroquois.

During my association with him in this present life he has given hints which, taken with various incidents, lead me to believe that the White Eagle who was once leader of the Six Nations of the Iroquois was in fact none other than Hiawatha, the mythical founder of the league. The name White Eagle by which we know him now signifies a spiritual teacher, and his principal concern is with brotherhood, to bring to men a true understanding of the meaning of brotherhood.

'White Eagle has not actually said he was Hiawatha, but there is a striking resemblance in character, personality and type of work between them. White Eagle's work through me today, and in past lives, has been to further the cause of peace and brotherhood. His messages during the past thirty years have been designed to prepare our minds for a new age of unity between nations.

'The American historian, Alvin M. Joseph, in his book THE PATRIOT CHIEFS, writes that Hiawatha is known to have received his training from a Master Deganiwidah, from whom he learnt, among other things, the principles of government which he embodied in the laws that constituted and governed the league.

'The way I came by the book, THE PATRIOT CHIEFS, convinced me that White Eagle wanted me to know more about his life as an Indian in North America. At the close of a Sunday service at the White Eagle Lodge in London, a stranger came up to me saying, "You must obtain the book on the patriot chiefs". I did so, and found in it historical proof of Hiawatha's existence and an absorbing account of his work among the Iroquois for the brotherhood of the tribes and establishment of the league. The book tells us, among other things, that Hiawatha called the union of the tribes, "the great white carpet of peace and brotherhood".

'Once during a performance of *Hiawatha* at the Albert Hall, I felt I was one of the Indians, and had to make an effort not to run into the arena with them. During the interval I sent a message asking if the only real Indian in the cast, Chief Oskenonton, who was playing the medicine man, would see me, and almost at once he was shaking me by the hand as if I was a long-lost relative, and exclaiming, "But you are one of my people!". I told him I had an Indian guide who had powerfully moved me to meet him, and he said that when he was singing his song to the dying Minnehaha, he had been entranced by the spirit of a great Indian chief. This, and other impressions, has convinced me that I was with White Eagle during his incarnation as Hiawatha.

'I believe that the unity of the six tribes remained strong through two centuries of conflict with the invading white man, until they finally suffered defeat at his hands. Yet its political institutions survived because the principles at the heart of the Six Nations' system were such that they are now included in the studies of those philosophers of Europe and America who seek juster and more humane methods of government. I believe the colonial leaders, dreaming of unity among English settlers, looked into the political organisation of the League. Iroquois leaders are known to have chided the colonists for not forming a union modelled on the League of the Six Nations.

'I quote again from THE PATRIOT CHIEFS. "In 1754 Benjamin Franklin's proposed Albany Plan of Union for the colonies drew direct inspiration from Hiawatha's League, and Franklin was not hesitant in reminding his fellow colonists that it would be a strange thing if Six Nations of ignorant savages should be capable of forming a scheme for such a union and be able to execute it in such a manner as that it has subsisted ages and appears indissoluble; and yet that a like union should be impracticable for ten or a dozen English colonies, to whom it is more necessary and must be more advantageous, and who cannot be supposed to want an equal understanding of their interests! It would be impossible to trace more than an indirect influence of the Iroquois League, via the liberal philosophers of the eighteenth century, on the United States government as it was constituted in 1789. But in such forms as the methods by which Congressional, Senate and House conferees work out bills in compromise sessions one may recognise striking similarities to the institutions of the great council fire of the League, which, despite the corrosive surroundings of the white man's civilization, the Iroquois people still faithfully maintain at their present-day 'capital' near Brantfor, Ontario. Even more genius, however, can be credited to the humanitarian Iroquoian conceptions of brotherhood and peace, for they were devised and achieved by Hiawatha for 'stone-age savages' before the coming of the white man, and they are still earnestly yearned for by the parliaments and United Nations of the twentieth-century humanity.".

'I turn now to a strange incident that is described in the book, AN ENCYCOLPAEDIC OUTLINE OF MASONIC, HERMETIC, CAB-BALISTIC AND ROSICRUCIAN SYMBOLIC PHILOSOPHY, by Manly P. Hall. "It was during the evening of July 4th 1776 that in an old State house in Philadelphia a group of men were gathered for the momentous task of severing the last tie between the old country and the new. It was a grave moment, and not a few of those present feared that their lives would be the forfeit for their audacity. In the midst of the debate, a fierce voice rang out. The debaters stopped, and turned to look upon the stranger. Who was this man who had suddenly appeared in their midst and transfixed them with his oratory? They had not seen him before, none knew when he had entered, but his tall form and pale face filled them with awe. His voice ringing with a holy zeal, the stranger stirred them to their very souls. His closing words rang through the building: 'God has given America to be free', and the stranger sank into a chair exhausted. Wild enthusiasm burst forth. Name after name was placed upon the parchment. The Declaration of Independence was signed, but where was the man who had precipitated the accomplishment of this momentous task, who had lifted for a moment the veil from the eyes of the assemblage and revealed to them a part at least of the great purpose for which the new nation was constituted? He had disappeared, nor was he ever seen again, nor his identity established."

'It seems clear to me that the Master who guided and taught Hah-Wah-Tah, Is-ra and Hiawatha played a part in the making of the constitution of the United States of America. Was he not the unknown man?

'In the early days of the White Eagle Lodge, at the end of a Sunday service, a stranger was introduced who said she had been urged to give me a small golden coin that White Eagle wished me to keep as a token of our joint work. It was a half-dollar gold piece in a design that was struck to commemorate the Constitution of 1789, on one side the head of a North American Indian, similar to White Eagle, on the other an eagle with the words, "In God We Trust". She said further that during the service, while I was speaking, she had seen beside me one whom she described as a man in the prime of life, with a fine, intellectual face, Vandyck beard and moustache, clothed in velvet doublet and hose of the Tudor period. This exactly fits the personality once known as Francis Bacon, who, I have reason to believe, is another personality of the Master and

Teacher who works with White Eagle as a Master once worked with Hah-Wah-Tah, Is-ra and Hiawatha. I feel sure he used this woman to send this American coin as a small proof that he has been behind White Eagle's work and my own during many lives, and behind the foundation of societies that work for peace among the nations.

'I should add that just as I finished the account of this incident, and as if in confirmation of my thoughts, a registered package was delivered, quite out of the blue, which contained a President Kennedy commemoration coin. Again the motto, "In God We Trust" appears on it, and on the reverse side the eagle.'

In the present day of life, White Eagle used Grace Cooke as a trance medium, beginning this work with her in her early twenties, and continuing right through her life until just a few years before her passing in 1979. For his work with her at that time he manifested mainly in the North American Indian personality she has described in the foregoing section. However, as White Eagle himself says, the white eagle itself is a symbol of the new Age of Aquarius, the age of spirit, the age of the brother–sisterhood of all life. He comes to remind us of the need for simplicity and purity of life and to revere Mother Earth. In a number of past lives he incarnated at times when returning to a simple way of life was really important for those embracing a spiritual way of life.

Many of those who are closely associated with White Eagle's work today recognise his personalities linked with the major religions of the world. For example, it is believed he had more than one incarnation linked with Islam and Sufism, and also with Taoism, Tibetan Buddhism and Zen as well as Christianity. In the present time, White Eagle often appears in a universal guise, not linked to any one particular personality.

Long before the dawning of the Aquarian Age, with its ideals of equality and brotherhood–sisterhood, White Eagle was pioneering these concepts in both religious and social areas. He has worked many times to break down the old Piscean Age barriers of class, colour, creed and gender.

A most important point about White Eagle to mention is his blue sparkling eyes, which always twinkle and convey love and a deep spiritual understanding. No matter what personality he dresses in, his eyes always seem to be the same. Whatever the form he chooses on any given occasion, whether it is a high priest of the Egyptian mysteries, a teacher from far ages ago in the Andes, or a simple Tibetan monk, his message contains the same universal truths that are common to the world's religions.

Let us end with his own words. 'We would remind you that all esoteric truths spring from the one simple truth. We would like you to see this truth as a tree—a tree of knowledge, shall we call it?—planted in the infinite and eternal garden. That tree has many branches, big branches breaking up into smaller ones and even smaller and smaller, until you get a very fine skeleton of the tree. These branches are the innumerable aspects of esoteric truth. But individual men and women get hold of one little branch, or even one little twig, and think that they have the whole truth and it is the only truth! By doing so, they are enclosing themselves in a little dark box, which we will call the mind, and it becomes a very dark prison. Slowly, however, each man or woman is touched in their heart by the love of God and, even more slowly, awakens to the truth of the unity of all life and religions.'

Jenny Dent
New Lands, Liss, April 2006

Author's Introduction

PART I of this book recounts my memory of a time when I was Minesta, daughter of an Indian chief of the Mayan race living thousands of years ago in a valley the Indians called Willomee, which means peaceful valley.

A series of small events in my most recent life points clearly to the possibility of my having been closely connected with the Indians and indicates a continuation through successive incarnations of the work I was engaged in at that time. There is even a continuity of features and physical characteristics. For instance, I have often been taken for an American Indian because of a dark skin, very dark brown eyes and black hair. Twice, when meeting Indians unknown to me, they have exclaimed, 'But you are one of our people,' and I felt certain this was true. Some years ago, on first meeting an Englishwoman who became my friend (she was the first white woman to travel down the Amazon in a canoe with South American Indians), she said she immediately recognized my connection with them and gave me a figurine taken from the tomb of an ancient Mayan chieftain that she believed really belonged to me.

These memories came through the higher mind. They did not come through automatic writing, dreams, trance-messages or any other form of mediumistic communication. They came by 'tuning-in' to a super-normal consciousness and steady thinking back into the past. It was an arduous creative effort, not of what is called imagination but of memory, to recover a past that is imperishable in the soul.

When I first wrote a description of my life as a Mayan girl in the book called PLUMED SERPENT (1942) which suggested that a distinctive Mayan civilization flourished at least ten thousand years ago in South America in the foothills of the Andes, it was objected, first, that the Mayas belonged to Central not South America and that the remains of the civilization called Mayan date back no further than the period A.D. 350-900. It is not part of my concern to prove or establish the factual accuracy of memories, which rests on a different basis, but I can at least claim that since then evidence has come to light which tends to support the assertion that a remarkable civilization, appropriately called Mayan, flourished many thousands of years ago in the Andean region that supplies the Amazon.

These discoveries tend to corroborate my story. At least it would seem, as a matter of observed fact, that at a time far in the past there was a civilization in what is now Peruvian jungle that had features similar to those of the civilization in Central America now known as Mayan.

On July 20th, 1965, White Eagle said:

'In years gone by, we endeavoured to bring through to you by impression, and in the dream-world, and by direct contact, certain details about the life of the ancient American Indian. We told you what would be discovered by explorers in South America, and that archaeologists would excavate the remains of the ancient American Indians, which would prove the truth of our words. We think it is true to say that the Indian culture goes back ten, fifteen, twenty, thirty thousand years and more. There still remain traces in the wilds of southern and northern America of monoliths, temples and settlements where Indian people live; and when the stones and hieroglyphs can be read much will be revealed. At present scholars cannot decipher the truths that the monuments disclose, as they cannot decipher the mystery you call Stonehenge. Some day, when human kind are ready for it, they will learn a great deal about the builders, but today scholars would neither believe nor take the trouble to investigate. Science is built on what is called fact, something that can be 'proved'. Why? Because your scientists have not yet developed certain faculties, certain areas of the brain, and do not really know what proof consists of. When through ethical and spiritual discipline humanity has reached the level at which powers, at present locked in the brain and nervous system can respond, people will comprehend and wisely use what those in the spirit-world can convey by impression on the parts of the brain in question.

'The details of the culture of the Indians are unknown because, as we have said, human kind cannot yet interpret the signs. The only dependable records are those that are called 'the akashic records'. Thought, sound and action are all impressed on the akasha, or the ether, and the only way really to discover truth about ancient races and prehistory is to develop the gift to read the akashic records.

'Try to forget all you have read and heard about savage Indians living in wigwams; not all the Indians were nomadic. The Indians of whom we speak had beautiful buildings, lovely temples, fine houses and stone buildings. The Indian culture goes back a long, long way before any known historical or archaeological records of the ancient Mayan civilization. The same culture known to these great Indian peoples can be traced to India among records relating to the ancient continent of Mu. Stone tablets in the archives in Nepal give the story of the flood and the ice age, together with all that happened to the surface of the earth and the peoples and races of those ancient times. They are recorded in certain places in the Himalayas, away from prying eyes, and the records corroborate what you will read for yourself when you are able to understand and read the etheric or the akashic records.

'You will notice that the figures depicted on the stones of the ancient Indian temples wear feathers, some of them at the back of the head: this is because to win a feather the 'brave' must show a certain moral as well as physical, a spiritual or, if you like, psychic quality that is centred at the back of the brain and enables him to function at a higher level. It is by this very sensitive centre that we work when we speak through a medium.'

There was a time, White Eagle tells us, when the Indians who had achieved a high degree of spiritual knowledge and power and respect were called 'Plumed Serpents'. These Plumed Serpents were what we today would call Elder Brethren or Masters. The crown of plumes they wore symbolized the state of illumination they had attained. More about these illumined ones will be found in the final chapter of this book.

The reader may question the brother–sister marriage described in the Maya story. Although I did not know it at the time, I learnt later that among the Mayas as among the Egyptians, who adopted their rites and social customs from the Mayan race, brother-sister marriage was usual, at least in the royal houses; this, significantly, seems also to have been the case in Peru. The idea may be repugnant today, but the laws governing marriage, like personal morality, are to some extent a function of time and place. There are still tribes, remnants of great peoples, that have the custom: indeed, the theme occurs in myth and legend from various parts of the world, as if brother–sister marriage had some mystical significance.It will be seen that in my Maya incarnation I was instructed by my father, Hah-Wah-Tah, in the fundamental laws of brotherhood in action. Hah-Wah-Tah in his turn was working under the direction of the Master in the mountain. In my Egyptian incarnation I was instructed by Is-ra (a reincarnation of Hah-Wah-Tah), once again the high priest, in the laws of brotherhood. Is-ra himself was guided by the Master (who appeared in a purple cloak). In a later incarnation, White Eagle was chief of a Mohawk tribe in the League of the Six Nations. I believe he was also the legendary Hiawatha; I was again his daughter, and he too was instructed by a Master. Finally, in this present incarnation I am once again instructed to work for brotherhood as White Eagle's medium, and he in turn is again instructed by a Master whom we sometimes call the Wise Knight, who incidentally usually appears to us with a purple cloak around his shoulders. To me this is a remarkable story, and it shows the continuation of the work of the White Brotherhood beyond the veil to spread 'the great white carpet of peace and brotherhood' over the world.

The Cave in the Mountains

IT IS unusual for anyone to attain material advantage or advancement without hard work and effort; the same rule applies to spiritual attainment. Nothing comes to the slothful, but treasure beyond all price waits for the ardent soul who will press forward in its search for truth.

When I think of spiritual unfoldment, I visualise the Sphinx which, part-quadruped, part-bird, part-human, symbolizes the power of the human spirit to rise on wings of meditation away from earthliness into spheres of consciousness which embrace all knowledge, all wisdom.

This symbol is common to the people of Atlantis, to the Mayas, the Egyptians and other ancient peoples. The winged beast, winged human being or winged sun are found in temples still extant in various parts of the world. One of the monoliths in the stone circles at Carnac in Brittany takes the form of a huge bird or winged beast. From all these signs we may infer that during life on earth a man or woman is meant to rise from the earth nature into the highest mysteries. The mystery schools of all ages have imparted the knowledge, which has to be earned by purity of life, that enables us to soar to higher worlds; but such journeys of the soul can only be attempted after much work and constant application. Some of the lessons confront us in daily experience, others come in course of the soul-discipline that is exacted before initiation. But when consciousness is free of the lower nature, the soul is free to explore a timeless universe. It experiences the joys of lives in higher worlds, and is able to bring the memory of these experiences back to earth. Poets and philosophers, sages and saints of all ages have travelled in the realms of light and recorded the truths they found there.

*

I was first instructed in the correct method of meditation by a teacher from the East who so infused my soul with his light and power that I learnt how to rise through the head chakra into the subtler worlds and to read there the etheric records of lives long past. When no such teacher is available, it is more difficult for the aspirant to pass consciously and quickly into a superior state. The mind must first be stilled, a state of inward peace be realized. There must be an awareness of the presence of God—or of pure love within the innermost being. The body should be upright, hands folded over the solar plexus, or with the tips of the curved fingers resting in the centre of the breast at the level of the heart. Breathing should be rather deeper than usual. With each intake of breath the aspirant should visualise a ray of the pure white light entering the body, as from the heart of a sun or star, and with the out-breathing see the outpouring of the great white light from the centre of the body. An unspoken prayer should rise from within the heart to enfold all of human kind in love and peace.

The consciousness of the one who is projecting such light and love is automatically raised, and the soul released from the limitations of its earthly mind can rise through the astral into the mental and celestial states of being.

After long practice in meditation, I was taken by White Eagle to his home. I seemed to rise like a bird and together we travelled up and up through mist to what seemed a tremendous height. Then the mists cleared and we were at the edge of a great lake, a little after sunrise. Now the air was crystal; the sun warmed the ground and ourselves. Mountains rose sheer from the lake, and early morning shadows gave promise of radiance to unfold with the day. Silence and peace were in our souls.

A canoe made of birch bark and with gracefully curved ends awaited us at the water's edge. We stepped in and glided over blue water so clear that the bottom of the lake could be seen. Another world danced before my eyes, for down there in the water grew plants with tiny flowers; and there were many coloured stones, glistening like gems. Then I looked up and saw pine trees on the shore towards which we were moving; they grew in dark green clumps up the mountainside, and I could just see a silver path winding among them. 'Before we attempt the climb,' White Eagle said, 'we will seek rest and refreshment.' He took me by the hand and led me to a cave, a resting-place of silver sand strewn with moss, tiny plants, and exquisite shells, where two places were hollowed into the shape of a human form, and there were pillows of green moss for the head. A spring trickled through a natural channel and drained into the lake. We cupped our hands and drank from this crystal stream.

Sitting in the entrance we gazed over the still lake, absorbing the light that poured from all nature. I felt I wanted nothing more than to remain in this beautiful place. 'Is this heaven?' I asked.

'It is heaven for you just now', White Eagle replied. 'But heaven is vast. You may discover many heavens; indeed, any place where you find perfect harmony and realize your at-one-ment with the cosmos is heaven'.

'Then we needn't go far from earth to find it?'

'No. Heaven is a state of conscious happiness, realized in different degrees in the soul. It is anywhere where you are happy according to the measure of your consciousness. You may think that heaven is a long way off, but God meant that human kind should live in heaven while still on earth. In fact, in creating life God put humanity in a state of bliss. It is sad that men and women have lost the secret and must now spend countless ages trying to find it again.'

'Will they succeed, having fallen so low?'

'They will. But only through the pain and the joy that human love brings. People wonder why God permits suffering; the reason is that through suffering the human spirit is awakened and the long adventure of the return to heaven begins.'

'I suppose the path is lonely, White Eagle?'

'No, my child, not all the time. There are places where the companions of your spirit may join you, places where the soul may rest for quite a long while in communion and supreme happiness.'

*

We set ourselves to the path and when we had climbed some distance I began to see what he meant. Looking back I saw lives I had lived. Some were blessed by human companionship when I had given healing, beauty and happiness to the world, while some were dark and sunless, utterly selfish lives and sad. 'Yes', said White Eagle, reading my thoughts, 'it is a pity that people should miss so much through self-will.'

We climbed on. White Eagle took me in my meditation to snow-clad heights where light enfolded us. Now I found myself in the Master's ashram, in a T-shaped room one end of which was arranged as a shrine, while the longer, wider part, with a window that faced the shrine, was furnished like a study, the walls lined with books, a Persian rug on the floor. A round tea-table was set with Chinese bowls, and I noticed one or two chairs of Chinese design, one especially of exceptional grace in which a Tibetan sat in deep meditation before the shrine. He was clothed in a Buddhist monk's robe, yellow, significant of his Order. His face expressed unassailable peace, unfathomable wisdom, a charming humour. Before him stood a life-sized golden Buddha. I saw not only the dense metal but an etheric light that streamed from the figure with such warmth that it was like fire. The Tibetan remained in contemplation for a time, and then, returning to ordinary consciousness, rose and came forward with hands outstretched to greet me as an old friend. Though I was getting better accustomed to my surroundings he must have seen that I was affected by the power and beauty of this place and he did all he could to make me at ease and happy in his presence.

In response to a signal a servant appeared and busied himself pouring tea into the bowls. He withdrew and I was invited to sit opposite my host, who handed me a bowl of the golden liquid. I have never tasted such tea before or since—it was a magic draught. As I sipped it I felt light glow in my heart; my body relaxed and felt light and strong; heaviness and strain disappeared and life pulsated through me. I could think with perfect clarity, and room, books, and furniture, had greater harmony, new beauty. With his right hand under my left elbow my friend raised me to my feet and guided me to the window. 'What you see', he said, 'is a manifestation of the eternal presence of those great ones who guard and govern earth. Behind all heat and passion, behind the beauty, joy and sorrow of humanity's evolving life, is the eternal, ineffable Father–Mother, while lesser gods live age after age among those silent peaks, far removed from the clamour of those plains where people kill one another, watching the human world. These are the agents of God's law by which men and women evolve from unconsciousness to God-consciousness. Their power is the power of the Supreme, but they never interfere with the action of human will, never step in to prevent mistakes, for it is through these that a person comes to know life on earth and in heaven, learns to know himself or herself. The gods see in humanity's pain a gradual evolution of the individual and collective spirit. They see races born and die, nations rise and fall, cycles revolve. They watch the ceaseless coming to earth of myriads of souls, their rise to the peaks of perfection, and then, the purpose of incarnation accomplished, their release and their passing on to freedom. Experience has brought these souls to God-consciousness, the final prize won after countless years in earth's toils.'

He fell silent, and we entered into the rhythm of the AUM, the sound out of which life comes, into which it returns, the Word in whose heart is that which alone can give the human being completion. We seemed to be part of the stream of life, the absolute consciousness. The ages were open to my sight. I saw the waxing and waning of religions, the rise and degeneration of cultures, watched science unfolding its secrets and continents crumbling into the sea. I saw the cycles that are completed and humanity struggling through it all to the light.

After the vision had faded my friend, asked if after what I had seen I found my own life on earth with its limitations and hardships worthwhile. I said I felt humbled and deeply grateful to have been created part of God's glorious kingdom—how could the smallness of everyday life find place in one's thoughts in face of the cosmic grandeur?

'Now you understand', he said, 'why your guides assure you so often that all is well.'

*

I came to know the resting-place on the mountain as the Cave of the White Cross and often found my way to it without White Eagle's help. But I never fail to find him awaiting me at the entrance and this is always the starting-point of voyages into the spirit world.

We go by the silver path up the mountain, but the effort of climbing is nothing compared to what it would be in the physical body, more like ascending by funicular. It has often reminded me of the fairytale in which Jack runs up his beanstalk and comes to the giant's kingdom. I seem to mount in an invisible carriage and arrive in a new world—not always the same, but life there shows what life on earth might be. It is almost impossible to describe, a state of consciousness, not merely fanciful but a state in which spirit animates all the events of a life that has been and is still being lived.

White Eagle and I have often climbed the mountain and found ourselves in a life lived on earth long ago. An archaeologist pieces together scattered facts and constructs an account of a vanished system of living and it is not disputed. Why should not the past be reconstructed out of fragments students find during their exploration in higher realms of consciousness? We are told, and we believe, that nothing in the universe is lost. Every atom of matter is retained, it merely changes form.

These glimpses of the past such as I have been privileged to obtain are not mere flashes of recollection that come and are lost. I can recover them. I am reunited with friends of past lives and sometimes I recognize them as companions in this present life. The past is not the closed book it is thought to be; memories of it are woven into our 'now'. It is surely helpful that a subtler consciousness should be awakened in us, throw brighter light on ourselves as we are and give us incentive to further effort.

'It is selfishness', White Eagle says, 'that bars the way to the mysteries. It is materialism that closes the golden gate into the world of reality'.

*

A day came when we ascended the mountain and entered the Universal Temple. I know no words adequate to describe the grandeur, beauty or solemnity of this Universal Temple. I can only say that I thought at once of graceful birches whose trunks form columns and whose branches make the fine tracery of the roof. A profound silence enfolded us. We had views of far, celestial places through windows patterned by trees; indeed, it seemed as if the windows gave magic to my sight, for I could see into realms of greater and greater glory.

By the time I had become attuned to my surroundings a number of people had gathered. I did not know them at first, but as memory began to stir I recognized each one as a friend of this present life on earth; moreover, I knew them now as true companions of my spirit through ages on earth and in heaven.

And then I was taken to witness a rite that is conducted perpetually for the souls of those who are ready for initiation into the White Brotherhood. We stood before a grand altar ablaze with golden light, and when I could bear to gaze at it I saw the figure of Christ, from whose heart (as it were) a fine golden rod reached out and twined about my wrist like a golden cord, binding my hand closely to my companion's. Then I saw on the altar a chalice that was enveloped in light, the Holy Grail; this was lifted without hands to my lips and I held true communion with Christ and the brother to whom the golden cord bound me. And now, being quickened in consciousness, I discerned the misty yet dazzling forms of the Brothers–Sisters of the Great White Lodge who filled the Temple with their radiance.

Now I saw clearly that when souls are united in the bond of real brotherhood neither time nor distance, death nor any change, can separate them. Again and again through the ages they meet and remember each other, if but dimly on earth. In fact we are forever one family and what is done by one, whether good or evil, affects the whole. Most important it is then that brothers and sisters fall into line with the master-plan of the Architect of the universe. Master-builders in His–Her service, they must not fail to work out on earth His–Her design for the regeneration of human kind. Now the black and white, the good and evil, in my own past lives stood out and I suppose the black and white squares on the floor where we stood for initiation symbolized this.

It was while in this raised state of consciousness that with the help of the 'Illumined Ones' I was taken back in memory to a life I had lived as an American Indian of the Maya race. This experience brought recollections of a series of events; and as I recall the memory of my companions and the incidents of this former life, I realize that I was laying then the foundation for my whole life's work. By 'whole life' I mean the continuation of the life of my soul through subsequent incarnations. This is why I was given the power to recall these memories. In this day of life I recognize some of my companions and brethren of those Mayan days, and they are still working with me for the fulfilment of the divine plan to re-awaken in human kind the lost secrets of the Ancient Wisdom. My memory of past lives is intended to show that the 'Illumined Ones' are still guiding and helping the spiritual evolution of humanity.

THE STORY

PART I

PLUMED SERPENT

Chapter 1

Minesta's Home

MANY thousand years ago, in the valley of a tributary of the Amazon, under the Andes, lived certain early Mayan-Indian tribes. Little is known about these ancient people, their history, customs and civilization, yet on occasion I can recall the main incidents of my life there as vividly as I remember things that happened in childhood in this present incarnation. Indeed, for some reason, scenes from the long past stand out in greater perfection of form, colouring and detail than experiences of my present incarnation. The further off in time the clearer the memory.

I do not know how long it takes for the climate and vegetation of a landscape to change, but I see my valley in a semi-tropical country beneath deep blue skies, a land rich and peaceful like the Garden of Paradise, and the great river was, I am sure, the Amazon. We called the valley Willomee, which means 'the spirit of peace is ever with us'.

My father's home was a long, low building in white stone, of unusual design, with many oblong windows and doorways steeply angled to form a triangle. Stone carvings decorated much of the building, particularly around the doorways and windows, while flowering vines climbed over the porticos. Many kinds of fruit hung in clusters on bushes and trees that grew in walled courts that surrounded the house. In fact, this home of mine could be described as a palace, for my father was chief and king. The family, which consisted of my father and mother with their five children, lived in the main building at the centre.

I remember my mother as a woman of rare beauty, gentle, wise, loving and beloved of everyone. In those days, the mother was revered in every household throughout the land, the king's wife and mother of his heirs especially, for she was thought to be endowed with the attributes of the Mother-aspect of the Supreme One. My mother, herself daughter of the chief who preceded my father, had been reared and trained in the arts and graces befitting her calling; the course of spiritual training she underwent was unusually severe, although wisely and lovingly conducted. I was the eldest daughter and named, after her, Minesta. Then came a brother, two sisters and, last of the family, my brother To-waan who, as I shall explain, held a place of honour in the household as co-heir to the throne.

The palace overlooked the homes of our Indian community, nestling along the valley and on the mountainside. From my favourite seat on the steps that led to an inner courtyard of the chief's residence I could see groups of small houses in white stone built on similar lines to those of the palace, each with carvings round the window-frames and each with the angled doorway. Shrubs and creepers were trained about the walls, while fruit bushes, fruit trees and vines flourished in the gardens.

The royal demesne extended across the valley and up the mountain for a considerable distance. Many landworkers, builders, scribes, household servants, clothesmakers, weavers, as well as priests and temple-servers lived on the estate, each with their stone house and piece of land. The settlement was not unlike a large garden city, vivid in colour and beauty.

The valley was often carpeted with wild flowers. In season, there would be small wild irises in many colours, although blue predominated in patches, their colour enhanced by the background of snow-capped mountains, purple and dusky blue. The soil was rich, with abundant harvests of corn and green vegetables, while the broad river teemed with fish and animal flesh was available for those of the tribe who ate meat.

Both men and women adorned themselves with jewellery, often splendid and of fine workmanship, according to their rank. The people took great pride in their appearance and were by no means crude or savage in dress or custom. The women in particular were beautifully clad in robes of rich colour, the dyes for which were obtained either from the roots of herbs and bushes, or from the bark of trees, or sometimes from crushed berries of various colours, sometimes from lichen that grew on the rocks. The arts and handicrafts of those days would compare favourably with those of the present time in quality and design.

The Indians brought many kinds of sparkling stone with varying colours and brilliance from caves, clefts and mines in the mountains, and these were lavishly used in the decoration of temples and halls of learning or initiation. Some of the bowls, mugs and plates we used in our home had been carved, ground and polished from one solid block of precious or semi-precious stone, richly-veined, full of colour and beauty. Other utensils were carved from beautifully grained woods, or moulded by hand from clay on the riverbank and baked. Pieces of rarer craftsmanship were hand-painted and varnished, or glazed by baking in clay ovens, heated over charcoal ablaze in a forced draught. Metals, especially gold, were melted in small crucibles over a furnace and the metal poured into sand moulds to make cups and bowls for tableware on formal occasions.

One stone, similar to what we call chalcedony, was held

especially sacred, possessing, it was thought, an exceptionally magnetic power that could draw down the blessing of the Great White Light. Whole altars were hewn from huge blocks of this blue stone and embellished in certain cases with gems of a different hue in the form of symbols representative of some spiritual influence which could work an immense effect on a worshipper's physical, mental and spiritual condition.

A symbol used more frequently than any other was the triangle in a circle. This represented the Father–Mother God and their Son, the triune Deity within the circle of universal love. The wedded life of a man and woman blessed with children was held symbolic of the triune Godhead; the trinity of man, woman and child, image of three in one, was thought godlike, blessed and sacred. This is perhaps one reason why in later times the system of morality practised by the North American Indians was recognized as an outstanding quality in the character of a noble race.

Such was the framework in which the picture of my life in southern America is set. Strangely, I look back to it without any sense of its being remote, but rather with a vivid thrill as if it were part of my being in an eternal now in which I lived, am living and shall live again.

Sometimes I see myself as a child, playing with other golden-skinned children; or as a maid sitting at my embroidery, the love of which remains with me (one of my rare hobbies today is embroidery and tapestry work). Later still, I am undergoing temple training, learning the arts of wisdom, just rule and leadership. I look again and the years bring me to marriage, motherhood, maturity. Then comes the autumn of my days and in time the laying-down of my physical body. And at last I am crossing the bridge into the hereafter, to rest and refresh myself for the next 'day of life' on earth.

Chapter 2

Minesta and Hah-Wah-Tah

AMONG all my memories, I see my father's beloved face the clearest. Yet I have no power to describe it, except to say that his features were regular, his mouth wide and humorous, showing unusual strength even in repose. Neither can I describe his eyes otherwise than by saying that they were extraordinarily kind and gentle, with a decided twinkle in their depths. I hardly ever saw them blaze with anger, but when they did no one dared disobey him. Perhaps the most unforgettable thing about him was his voice, low, musical, seldom raised, yet every word perfectly clear. No-one could ever forget its cadence or lose the love and confidence it inspired; there was a quality, a grace and power in it as in the speaker himself. People did not fail to hear the least word when Hah-Wah-Tah spoke.

He usually wore a loose robe the colour of the sun's light, simply embroidered at the neck, and on the edge of the wide sleeves with mystic symbols. From a cord round his neck hung an exquisitely carved amethyst, a cross in a circle about four inches in diameter: he was never without this jewel. About his brow he wore a golden circlet with the symbol of the 'All-seeing Eye' in the centre; but on ceremonial occasions the circlet was replaced by an elaborate headdress like a crown of soft, white feathers, twelve inches or more in height, while jewels of different colours, each of occult significance, hung in clusters of seven over the ears.

The name, Hah-Wah-Tah, meant a wise man or spiritual leader, one who is dearly loved. He bore himself with grace, kingly yet humble, wise yet childlike. He governed with the vision of the Sage, and this is why his people were happy and contented; why for the most part they spent their lives in peace, each contributing to the general welfare. Each family had its home and land in the valley or on the mountains, where they lived not so much for themselves as for the happiness of the community. A person who grew into fuller wisdom and achieved a position of authority through the development of his gifts was honoured for progress in self-discipline and spiritual grace.

Willomee became a home of peace and harmony through the teaching of the White Brothers, the Plumed Serpents, who during these years revealed to Hah-Wah-Tah's illumined vision many secrets relating to the power and influence of sun, moon, planets and constellations. These, in course of time, he handed on to his children, who were enjoined to use them for the blessing of human life. He was known throughout the territories of the Mayas as a king of peace and brother to all. Travellers came from far off to listen and learn of him concerning the mysteries of life, death and the hereafter; and no one ever left his presence without some jewel from Hah-Wah-Tah's store of wisdom.

He ruled with unwavering justice over the lesser tribes, people who are now assumed to have been savage and warlike, but this was not so in those days before people of darkness brought on the tribes sorrow, suffering and all the ills that attend the powers of evil.

I remember him in the pride of manhood, clad in the wisdom and power of maturity. I remember him white-haired, but never bowed under life's responsibilities. I shall always think of him as a man great and gentle beyond all others, with room in his heart for many another's pain, and kindness enough to renew the whole earth.

One morning I specially remember, when from far off I watched his tall figure greet the dawn outside the door of our home, hands raised in salutation to the rising sun and to the Great White Spirit of his world and his people. No morning passed without his giving thanks in this manner to Father, Mother and Son, the triune One whom he worshipped. And this morning he seemed as he stood there in simple dignity to personify a Son of God, a man truly made in God's image.

*

One day I saw my reflection in still water, a graceful Indian girl whose black hair, braided in two thick plaits falling over her shoulders, had a rich sheen. She wore a simple white tunic fringed at the knees and shoulders in the usual Indian style. The olive skin, tinged faintly with copper, was enhanced by the whiteness of the dress and the blackness of the hair. Neck and arms were adorned with necklaces or armlets of vivid beads or stones, and my reflection wore a gold circlet around the brow, with one splendid jewel at the centre of the forehead, a precious stone found in the high Andes and used by the wise ones of the tribe for their temple altars. The wearing of this stone meant that I had inner or spiritual vision.

Such was my appearance in those days. As to my nature, I remember that whenever I met a stranger I would avert my gaze, although I felt neither timidity nor strangeness in my heart but always a quiet, intuitive watchfulness of the ways of men and women and the life of lesser creatures of the woods and streams. I lived a vivid life in myself, close to the heart of things; and in my outer life I accepted joyfully all that the fair world brought me.

I must have been a strange child. Nearly all I knew and the wisdom I was learning came through my father's instruction; but the vision I gained by this means continually revealed strange things; it seemed to unveil nature's inner life, as it were the 'soul' of bush, flower and tree. I saw that the many things people think inanimate, even stones and boulders, the great mountains and earth herself, are manifestations of spirit.

Once at early morning, I wandered under a cloudless sky down to the river. My favourite seat by the river was a tree-trunk lying among wild flowers on the bank. Here I could listen to the music of springs that came welling through the rocks, and see waterfalls great or small, near or afar, spraying diamonds in sunlight. The stream came swirling from distant heights, dashing over huge boulders, leaping to kiss and bejewel the ferns and wild flowers on its way to the great river. In some places creamed with foam, flinging its sunlit spray aloft, in others it was swift, smooth and dark.

I could identify myself with these waters. They seemed to sing and echo in my soul. I could merge myself with the hastening streams as with the flowers, the little furry beasts and other creatures. My soul had its own power of flight and I could soar with the birds, brethren that shared with me the life given by the gods. Had I not learnt that pain or injury wantonly inflicted on any creature must in time bring like pain to myself?

Such was the philosophy I had from my father.

*

Hah-Wah-Tah would often join me beside the river and we would talk long or else sit in silence. I learnt much from this communion with him.

Waiting one day I saw him come striding down the path, his mien tranquil, happiness in his face. Soon he joined me. While I waited for him my attention was drawn to the little people—some call them fairies—at play among ferns and flowers, or to the water sprites that danced in foaming eddies, and the elementals busy among the rocks. One amusing little fellow had become a special favourite, a dwarf-like creature who seemed to come from nowhere, clad like the Mayas. Today he squatted on a rock near us.

'Who is this little man?' I asked my father.

Hah-Wah-Tah paused to focus his inner sight. 'He is an earth elemental. He and his like can live numberless years in the rock.'

'But where does he come from?'

'He probably lives in the rock where you so often see him. He is part of it, its life-force or spirit. I have told you that everything in nature, not only trees and flowers, water, wind, fire, the rain and the clouds but rocks and stones too, has its own life-spirit. And all the nature-spirits have affinity with ourselves, if we truly love and understand nature. They enjoy human companionship when it is friendly; it helps on their evolution to learn the ways of humanity and gain its affection.'

Can you imagine how wonderful, how thrilling, such information made the nature world to me? 'So that is why this elemental makes himself as like a little man as he can?' I asked. 'Why is he so solemn and interested? And why does he come so regularly when we two are here?'

'He knows we can see him, so he comes in the shape easiest for us to recognize. The human being is the highest form of earth-life, made in God's image, although God is the Father–Mother of all creatures. So when they know we are friendly and can see them—and they know it quickly—the nature-spirits take human shape. Your little man likes to be seen and recognized because whether he knows it or not he aspires to develop his life-consciousness through association with human friends.'

'Can they hear and understand us?' I asked.

'Oh yes.' We sat silent, watching the elemental, who now seemed somewhat embarrassed by our attention. One could almost say he began to melt into the rock. 'Oh don't go!' I cried, and he became clear again. 'Father, did you say he is part of the rock?'

'Yes. As your body is the house or temple in which your spirit dwells, so also is the rock your little friend's house. In and behind what you touch and see is a world finer and more beautiful, within interpenetrating without. Nothing in either world exists without a life-spirit in it, which is part of God, the Great Spirit or infinite Father–Mother. Nothing can exist or continue to exist—rock, stone or earth itself, bird, beast or human—unless spirit or life-force dwells in it and sustains it.'

There was a power in my father's words, gentle as they were, that seemed to sink into my memory and abide there, as if nature herself spoke her truths to me. I never forgot those moments in which the song of the stream, the hum of insects, the wind in the trees, formed part of a spell. Yet stranger far, was the unveiling of secret things.

Presently I asked Hah-Wah-Tah if my dear dwarf would die some day, as our human friends in the village must die.

'Nothing dies,' he replied. 'Nothing can ever die. Your little friend may pass into another form when he has finished with what he has now, but he will enjoy a more advanced condition. He may become a tree-spirit, but his essence can never die away. He will change, advance, evolve, growing in knowledge and understanding. As they are at present, these little people don't think as we can think; they feel as we can feel, but not with the same intensity. Their thinking is done for them.'

After a silence my father continued: 'Humans have power of free will. We can choose our thoughts, but the little people of the nature kingdom have to obey their ruler, who thinks for them. As a ruler in earthly kingdoms makes and enforces laws, so it is in the nature world. Men and women may call the nature-rulers angels, archangels or gods. Once humanity understands and grows friendly with its brethren of the nature Kingdom, they will co-operate in humanity's work and bring blessings; but if human beings are harsh or cruel towards others and nature, the nature brethren can impoverish or even destroy them. Brotherhood with all is the condition of happiness and plenty.'

Again silence fell and we drank in the beauty around us. Suddenly I pointed to where the water creamed and foamed and broke into spray. 'Look! Oh look! Fairies in the water, so tiny, so silvery! When sunlight catches them they are dressed like rainbows. They are having such fun, splashing one another. They hold tiny pipes to their lips, do you see? Are they playing pipe music? I can't hear it.' I tugged his sleeve. 'Do tell me what they are doing.'

Hah-Wah-Tah seemed to listen. 'Open your ears', he said, 'to the sound of the waters, the birdsong, the rustle of wind in the leaves. Listen hard, for underneath these sounds there is silence. Hear it and you will hear a rhythm, a harmony. Put your ear to the earth sometimes and you will hear earth's murmur. Go close to the waterfall and under the sound of splashing and rushing your inward ear will hear a secret rhythm. It is this that the water sprites accompany on their pipes. All the nature world is a rhythm, a song of God; and from this, this power, vitality, life-essence proceeds, and all things have their being in it. The clouds chant to one another as they soar above earth. Sunlight and rain bring down the heavenly sound and it echoes in all growing things and in the waters. All creation keeps time with the celestial harmonies. Life has its birth-time, maturity, decay, death, but the life that dwells in the form presses onward and ever evolves, ever unfolds. And these little creatures, fairies, gnomes and sprites, are necessary in human creation and evolution. They are the lesser brethren, the little people, ever ready and willing to help us. True, humans must learn to command them, not by sorcery and the black arts but by the magic of love. The secret of all creation lies in that mighty word.'

Now Hah-Wah-Tah sat musing. After a while he rose without further word, laid his hand on my head and went his way. I stayed where I was, entranced. On this day of wonders inner vision seemed more vivid than ever before and I watched the play of the myriad little folk without daring to move, hardly even to breathe. Grass, ferns, flowers, seemed alive with them, rustling, whispering, crowding on me with demonstrations of friendliness. And I saw other strange little beings among the rocks, busy with miniature tools. I could not see what they were at but I rather thought their work was a kind of make-believe designed to impress me with their importance. I listened to a myriad sounds that seemed to reach me not through my ears but another part of my head. I remember thinking that if I held my ears tight to stop outside noises I should hear the little people better. I did this…. Yes, I thought, the sounds are clearer. How I wonder what they are saying! Now I am seeing and hearing the little people in my mind. Yet they must be real if they have such important work to do, as my father says.

Now another kind of sound broke the spell and I turned to see my brother To-waan. The magic hour by the stream was over but this was joy indeed. I felt thankful to see To-waan again and ran to meet him, for had he not been away in far places for several moons, facing great dangers? When I found myself folded to his heart as in a lover's embrace my happiness was complete.

Chapter 3

The Brotherhood of the White Magic

TO-WAAN, my youngest brother, a stalwart young brave —few among the Mayas could match him in speed or skill—was going through the discipline required of him before he could succeed Hah-Wah-Tah. I had looked on him with tender affection since childhood, knowing he was to be my husband, when he would need my love as wife, counsellor and mother of his children. His splendid strength and skill stirred my heart with pride and admiration; and when he put on a superior way with me I smiled to myself, for without me his power to accomplish things would be small. I realized equally well that without his love and strength I could not live, for I too must undergo severe training and great ordeals before I should be thought fit to rule when the time came.

To-waan was just back from a journey made without companions and designed to test his strength, hardiness and skill to the limit. He had set himself to climb hitherto unscaled heights, to endure rigours of cold and exposure, and to track down and meet Brother Bear face to face and so to daunt him with the courage in his own heart that the bear would refuse combat. Such trials and tests were part of the training a young brave destined to be Chief must endure; for it was thought that a man who showed high and selfless courage in the flesh would be pure in spirit and resolute.

We seated ourselves on a log by the river and To-waan

unfolded his tale. 'I followed the river bed', he told me, 'until it lost itself among vast crags and heights I found I must scale. I climbed day after day, resting at night in some caves, sometimes climbing on the next day, sometimes going into great clefts out of which I must climb yet again, climb till at last I flung myself down on the ground and slept. This time when I woke the sun was high. I sat up and looked about me and found myself on the edge of a pine forest, whose trees shot skyward straight and tall like the columns of a temple. I scrambled to my feet and walked on through the pines, thinking of enchanted woods.

'Presently I came on a house or sanctuary built of stone, stone wrought into a strange, graceful design. It was amazing to find so beautiful a building on the crest of a wild and apparently unexplored mountain range; and then, as I gazed at it, a man came towards me, a man such as I had never seen, tall, wearing a white robe, curiously embroidered with gold, and on his head a crown of eagle's plumes. His face was more peaceful than I can tell you, with an indescribable light in his eyes and a cadence in his voice that made every word music.

'The stranger took me into his house', To-waan went on, 'and offered food and rest. Then he asked me to follow him to a shrine in the central court where other priests were busy at work of various kinds. "Do you remember this shrine?", he asked. I thought hard and could remember nothing, yet I knew I had been in this temple and met this man.

'"Years ago', he said, 'your father, Chief Hah-Wah-Tah, took the path you have followed, and scaled those crags with you, an infant slung across his back. He brought you to me and the Brothers of the White Light who live here."

'Then who are you?' I asked.

'I am known as Menes.' Menes means a wise man, as you

know. "I am a priest of the Plumed Serpent; and you, To-waan, were dedicated almost from birth as a server of the Brother-hood. Your father brought your sister Minesta here too and she likewise was dedicated to the service of the Light. You are to serve your people together."

"'Then it wasn't by chance that the path led me to these crags, through the pine wood and to the temple?" I asked.

"'No indeed. You obeyed the voice of the Spirit. You were drawn here irresistibly, yet it seemed to you that you came of your own free will."

'While Menes spoke I felt the magic power that radiated from him and from the entire place. Trees, flowers and grass seemed to pulsate with joyous life. The colours on that height were such as I had never seen in the country that surrounds us here. All nature was enriched, Minesta, more radiant, more beautiful, in that magic spot. Then Menes said, laying a hand on my shoulder. "I have something to show you." He led me to the edge of a precipice so high and wide that all the world seemed to spread out before me. He touched my brow and awakened a vision. Past and future were open to me.

'I looked across great plains that stretched from the roots of the mountains to wide seas and across the seas to an island continent, fertile land cultivated by many tribes while others gathered in fair cities with temples on every height. The people and land seemed bright at first, but then I looked deeper and saw corruption brooding in the temples, creeping into people's hearts, so that even the soil became unclean and I saw fire and destruction lurking under land and sea. Then flames dissolved the earth, mountains toppled and seas overwhelmed the cities, and I watched until a remnant, a few souls still pure in heart such as Menes, sailed from what was left of the heights, the tops of the highest mountains and the white temples that yet stood on them. They were saved because they still followed the White Magic, which means they had never put their magic power to base uses, always used it to bless and help human kind. Because they were selfless in service, they won salvation, while others, those who used the magic to gain dominion over the people, were swept away in the floods. The very power their sorcery had put subject to selfishness destroyed them.

'Now, with the vision Menes awakened in me, I watched the centuries unroll. I saw ships bearing the white magicians sail north, east and west, taking the secrets of their magic to peoples far across the world. Some went to a sun-baked desert land where a great river flowed; and an empire arose there, peopled by followers of the White Light. Hah-Wah-Tah and we too will live there, in a land called Egypt.

'Another ship sailed north to a small green island guarded by seas and cliffs where the priest of the White Magic landed among white-skinned people. An even more widespread empire will arise from this island, a chain of lands encircling the globe; and again we three shall live there. I saw that the knowledge and mystical truth the priests took with them will be seeds of power and wisdom from which this commonwealth of free peoples, this race that will colonise a world, will spring. From them will spring yet another race in a continent north of our own land.

'All this lies in the future. But when I looked again into the past I watched yet another ship sail west to the setting sun and Menes was in it with a companion and others dressed in white and gold. They made their way up a great river and built a temple by magic power on the heights. I knew Menes then as a man not subject to sickness and death, but one destined to live and rule among human kind during long centuries. I saw him as a master with strange powers. He sent rays of light and love to the very soul of any man, woman or child selfless enough to attract them, so that a soul once held in the ray would evolve and grow, take the steep path of initiation perhaps, and after severe testing, accomplish in one lifespan what might usually take many an incarnation. And some would remain unconscious of the ray, or deliberately reject the Master's help: decision lies with the individual, the choice is his or hers.

'I can't tell you, Minesta, how long I spent looking into past and future. I might have been in a trance that lasted days while I seemed actually to be living in that vision-world. It could have been only a short time—I can't say. But what I'm telling you so briefly seemed to last through a great space of time.

'It was over. Menes said we must go back to the temple. I stayed there many days with the White Brothers, and I shall never forget what I learnt from the communal life there, what I found during times of observation, times of communion with the worlds of spirit. But the day came at last when I was told that it was time for me to renew my life among human kind and put what I had learnt up there in the mountains to the test of experience. Before I left, I was summoned to the presence of the elder brother and priest and, kneeling before him, received my work for humanity as a solemn charge. Then with their blessing in my heart I said goodbye to Menes and the Brethren and came back to find you and our parents. Safely, with winged feet and joyous heart I came.'

'And to think,' I said, 'that we were both linked with this man of power and light, and with this temple, when we were babies! Does this account, do you think, for the gift of sight that sees behind appearances into nature and human hearts?

And I thought I was alone in this! I thought it was through my own powers that the worlds of light were open to me!'

To-waan told me later that at the appointed time a summons would come again and we should go with Hah-Wah-Tah to the temple. He didn't know how long we were to wait, but we must possess and prepare ourselves patiently till the call came. 'And now', he said, 'we have much to talk over with our father and mother.'

Chapter 4

Stone and Sun-Worship

TO-WAAN and I often talked about the Brotherhood living high up on the mountain in their sanctuary among stalwart pines, and waited as patiently as we could for the promised call to visit them with Hah-Wah-Tah. We thought of their tranquil lives, their ordered days spent studying the mysteries of the heavens and of the life of each soul. They conducted themselves by the laws of nature and the Plan of the Architect of the Universe as it had been revealed to them, that they might work for the evolution and progress of natural and spiritual life on earth. We thought about these souls with wonder and awe, working so patiently for the glory of the Great White Spirit, giving all the help in their power for the good of humanity.

Hah-Wah-Tah had indeed spoken wisely when he told us they were messengers sent by the Great White Spirit, Amaru, to teach us concerning the wisdom of the gods. For among other things they taught him that by obedience to the laws of brotherhood and upright living a person would receive power to control even the air-currents, and to direct the work of nature spirits to grasses, plants and trees, thus ensuring rich yields of fruit and corn to those who loved these beings. They had also shown lesser priests among the Mayas how to perform various rites and ceremonies that won help from the spirits of the five elements, Earth, Air, Fire, Water and Ether. Neither To-waan nor I were ever likely to forget the great gatherings of people who came from far and near at the time of the great seasonal feasts when all the tribes took part in ceremonial marches in a temple that stood above Willomee. Open to sun and wind and all the forces of nature, roofed by the sky, it dominated a plateau whose far horizon was a chain of snowy mountains. A double circle of great stones, weighing many tons, stood rooted deep in earth like immense columns, round an altar carved from the sacred blue stone that was said to have come from the sun. The stones of the outer circle had been exactly sited to represent the constellations and planets, so that the central altar symbolized the Sun the Mayas worshipped, within the band of the zodiac. Of course our people worshipped not so much the visible sun, whose warmth and light gave us crops and fruit, as an invisible, spiritual sun that was thought to be the soul or self of the visible sun. We worshipped as well, not so much the visible planets and constellations, as an angelic emanation or influence that we believed came from them; because such emanations or influences, from sun, planet or constellation, were thought to act directly in everyone's life, our ceremonies and rituals were designed to evoke these powers and centre them on the people. Thus worshipping nature, symbolized by the sun and the zodiac, we worshipped also the reality behind the appearance or material aspect of the heavenly bodies.

The great stones of the temple were erected by magic. No other means was possible, since many of them ran to scores of tons. It was believed that the constituents or elements of the stone, chiefly pure silica, were precipitated or called down by magic from the ethers that surround the earth, taking shape and position under control of those spirits that rule the mineral kingdom, working under command of the priests. Stones of this weight are still found in ruins along the Cordillera, a puzzle to engineers. The knowledge brought by the Holy Ones to the Mayas that so far exceeded that of the present day spread to Egypt and India to be used in the building of temples and pyramids there.

The three high priests of the temple at Willomee were appointed guardians of the Holy Light, in which spirit was centred. This Light did not arise from flame or burning substance; it was a manifestation or concentration within the stone of the central altar, lambent and beautiful by day and by night.

The principal ceremonies were seasonal, and all the tribes took part in them. A first procession entered the temple at the western opening, preceded by some bearing fruits, corn and spring-water, by others swinging censers in which sweet-scented herbs burned. On entrance, one half of the procession turned north-east, the other south-west, pacing in single file rhythmically. Thus two great circles of men and women, thousands of them, perambulated, one within the other, two wheels moving in opposite directions, in perfect rhythm. Chants of praise and thanksgiving to God were sung during the perambulations, which went on day and night, first in cycles of three times three, symbolizing the trinity, the power, wisdom and love of God: three times three, or nine, the number of the complete man or woman. Then a pause, a period of silent waiting, and once more the two circles would move, one against the other, in perfect rhythm. This time they went round five times, then again five times and yet again, each five rounds symbolizing and evoking the gods or kings of the five elements. Then again a pause, a waiting, while their power manifested in the hearts and souls of those taking part. Then again onward seven times seven, each round symbolizing, evoking, one of the seven angels of the seven planets. For it was believed that the planetary angels could actively help humanity: hence the sevenfold perambulation for the sevenfold reception of the angelic power. Then followed a twelve-times-twelve cycle, this time designed to call on the gods of the twelve constellations or signs of the zodiac and greet them, for such were believed to attend these gatherings. The bounty of earth and heaven, often so ungraciously accepted today by human kind, was then acknowledged with due dignity and praise. At seed-time, special prayer for plenty was made; at harvest-time acknowledgment to the lesser gods and the Infinite.

In this way Hah-Wah-Tah and all his peoples paid tribute to the power these natural forces hold in human kind's life and well-being. We believed without question that the little people helped us. In both the fire on the hearth and the campfire on the hills dwelt a beneficent salamander or fire-spirit, to whose kindliness we owed warmth and the flame that cooked our food. Every growing crop was nourished by myriads of tiny creatures under direction of their God: we thought it wise and well to co-operate with them and never to tempt them by rashness, self-assertion and harsh demeanour.

The Mayas worshipped a universal, impersonal, supreme Deity who showed four aspects of itself as a God of Love and a God of Power, a God of Good and a God of Evil, the De-stroyer. They were taught that destruction played an essential part in human evolution and in the universe; for evil tested each and every soul, working to eliminate what was weak and unworthy. It was God's pruning knife. They worshipped also lesser deities who seemed personal to them, all of whom had their being in the One; and they venerated the angels or gods who controlled the five elements.

On the days set apart for these Grand Chains the

ceremonial lasted from dawn to dusk and on through the night. Any who wearied were replaced.

One night To-waan awakened me and asked me to climb with him to the stone temple on the mountain standing over Willomee. A sound of chanting came through the darkness and we could see a glow of light high above us. When we reached the temple, the perambulating circles had come to a halt; all stood facing the central altar, which was now a block of light that flamed in the very heart of the stone. We slipped into our places and stood spellbound, watching the fire ceremony. From it, I believe that the campfire ritual of the North American Indians was derived.

We watched as three tall priests evoked the fire spirit with outstretched arms. At their feet lay a little heap of dried sticks and suddenly there appeared high overhead a spark of light that waxed and glowed. It hovered for a moment, then came down between their still, up-reaching hands to rest on the sticks, which burst into flames as the glowing spark touched them.

The perambulation was resumed. To-waan and I took our places in the chain and moved with the people in this unspeakably solemn rite. Hah-Wah-Tah had opened my eyes to the hidden powers of nature and I felt that the great ones who rule the little people, tall, impersonal, not unfriendly but mighty in power, had drawn very close. In my heart, I felt myself to be their child and had no fear; rather an indescribable love, a sympathy, an understanding of their patience and helpfulness that drew friendliness and co-operation from them.

How should there be anything but love and brotherhood on such a night! My soul swung into the rhythm, my heart soared with the chant. The beat of ten thousand feet, the song of a myriad voices, rose to the stars. Heavenly beings bent to bless us and the encompassing universe was friendly. The essence of Godhead permeated all things.

We perambulated the temple all night. The thousands moved in perfect rhythm, almost breathed and thought as one, while the bright stars seemed as if they too awaited a magical dawn. Then there came a faint grey light in the east that banded the horizon with layers of green and purple; rose-light crowned the mountains, rose deepened to blood-red on distant snows. Now every soul faced east with arms outstretched, hands open in welcome. Then suddenly the sun rose over the horizon and a new day was born, the day that would be rich in blessing from our life-giver and king.

Chapter 5

Minesta's Initiation

WITH SUCH rituals did the Mayas pay homage to the gods of heaven and earth, recognizing their true significance in the life of human kind and knowing that without their help human life would cease. The foregoing is a general description of the half-yearly ceremonies, to which all were summoned; but there were many others, some of which were held in the white temple above Willomee. Here, set in the altar front or reposing on it, were symbols that represented the planets and ancient signs of the zodiac, each carved in a precious stone whose colour was that of the planet or sign in question. The Sun blazed in pure gold studded at the centre with rubies. The Moon was wrought in silver, Jupiter in deep blue sapphire, Venus in turquoise, Saturn in emerald, Mars in amethyst, Mercury in flaming orange firestone. The twelve signs of the zodiac were arranged like the spokes of a wheel: Aries, pure red; Taurus, red-orange; Gemini, pure orange; Cancer, orange-yellow; Leo, pure yellow; Virgo, yellow-green; Libra, pure green; Scorpio, green-blue; Sagittarius, pure blue; Capricorn, blue-violet; Aquarius, pure violet; Pisces, violet-red.

Other assemblies were held in cave-temples in the mountains, to study the secret mysteries. Here too the priests trained neophytes for initiation into the lesser mysteries; that is, for the unfoldment of their innate powers, the spirit in heart and head, the God in them. The course was taken in three steps or degrees. A candidate for the first degree underwent training for seven years before he or she was thought ready to stand the severer tests. From first to second degree took three years more, and two more between second and third. Thus, it was seven years before any form of initiation took place, and twelve before the soul was thought fit to serve in the Brotherhood.

A candidate of either sex was eligible for this lengthy training. During the first seven years he or she must learn to control all personal desires and ambitions, so that the physical body, the nervous system, the emotional self and the brain were subordinated to the higher self. Among the terrifying experiences that the candidate had to face were the conditions in the lower astral worlds, through which some have to pass after death; while still living in a physical body he or she must endure astral tortures in the mind. The purpose of this was to achieve control of the physical, emotional and mental life by the higher self or first principle immanent in the heart.

In the process of training body and mind to obedience, sufferings and hardships of various kinds were inflicted in order to test the candidate's willpower in regard to the frailties of the flesh. One of the severest was the scorching of it over the altar fire. At first when the hands were bound and held over the flame the pain was excruciating; but in time the will so dominated the flesh that no pain was felt and no scar remained. Following at once on this came the ordeal of the ice-temple in which the candidate must remain all night. Such training protected the flesh from intense heat or cold and taught how the power of thought could be used to heal injuries suffered by accident or otherwise. Endurance is a quality that still ranks high with the North American Indian.

The candidate must also pass the test of courage, learning

to overcome fear of pain and suffering. And by long periods of abstinence must keep the sacred law of sex inviolate, usually while facing severe and subtle temptations. The Mayas did not enforce celibacy, but abstinence was ordained except at certain seasons when a man and a woman mated under direction of the gods of Venus, who were thought to control the building of the form-body on earth. These and other tests were repeated until the neophyte's will triumphed; but if it failed he or she was dismissed with ritual words which mean, 'Withdraw, Stranger, and pray to the God of the Sun to increase your strength'.

Although my girlhood came after the first Golden Age was over, the religious teaching in the White Brotherhood retained the principles that lead to human perfection, principles given out at the dawn of human life. The ideal held before the neophyte was the Archetype, true and perfect child of God

*

Not until I had passed tests of courage and endurance, learnt to control my impulses towards carelessness, laziness, self-indulgence and greed, and subdued my disposition to physical excess of all kinds including impurity, was I allowed to enter the temple and live there, now having the password that alone admitted a candidate. Thereafter I visited my family and people at rare intervals. Temples where candidates were trained were formed from a series of natural caves deep in the mountains. I lived here for three years, in a cave open to sunlight and air, overlooking a lake. Sometimes, very far away, I could see some of my people crossing the lake in canoes, or smoke from their campfires floating over the trees. I often felt a yearning for human companionship ; indeed I was very lonely. The school of initiation offered no easy discipline for body or soul.

During the three years between first and second degree, I

was taught daily by the priests and priestesses. Whereas preparation for the first degree largely concerned the body, its measure of endurance, strength and courage and its resistance to the temptation of ill-health, which for one on the path is but a form of slothfulness, I had now to face the subtleties of mental temptation. My earlier, girlish faith and trust in God's goodness was now assailed by anxieties, doubts, weaknesses and fears, so that the strength and certainty I once had seemed irrecoverable.

In preparation for the second degree I was taught to exercise my powers of observation and to use the courage learnt in physical ordeals. In the short space of three years I sought to gain a measure of mental and moral steadfastness and poise that without such discipline might have taken a whole life or perhaps several incarnations. And even when I returned to the world I had to spend long periods in study and meditation on the wonders and science of nature, observing the winds and air-currents, the clouds and their formation, for whole days and nights, learning to forecast the seasons and rainfalls. I learnt about the magic art of rainmaking as well, how to divert the air-currents so that they brought the clouds to any neighbourhood where they were needed. This was so that when To-waan and I came to rule over our people we should be able to foretell the weather and to advise and warn the people regarding the time to sow and to reap. I was also taught husbandry, the ploughing and preparation of the land, the sowing and reaping of the grain. To attain the second degree I must be proficient, by the priests' standard, in such arts and crafts as the welfare of the people demanded, including the growing and storing of food, the production of materials for clothing, their housing and the ordering of their lives.

We watched the constellations through long nights, studying

their influence on body and mind, on health and outlook, on the soul and spiritual evolution. Indeed, training for the second degree might be described as a course in natural science as applied to the ordering of human existence.

And now, having performed the labours and passed the tests required for the second degree, I felt ready to undertake the tests that led to a third and final initiation. For this I was taken to a cave high on the mountain and left there alone for a long time of silence and meditation. This was the subtlest and most difficult test of all. Although food and water were put in the cave at intervals, I spent weeks and months alone watching the sun rise and set and the seasons change. But this was the sharpest ordeal: I had to face legions of elementals and wrestle with them, to overcome or be overcome. Again and again, these creatures of the underworld tempted me with all manner of bribes to put myself in their hands, to surrender my faith and trust in God or eternal good. In return, they would bestow on me power to work the strange magics of the Lucifers, great powers over earth itself and its people, over the people of the inner world even. I passed whole days in mental torture, often feeling an agony of temptation, so that spent with the weariness of this mental and moral contest I seemed to be thrown into a pit of darkness far blacker than night and I lay on the floor of the cave as one dead.

But my heart still beat and I lived on, clinging desperately with heart and mind to the thought of God, to the light of the spirit of goodness I still felt within me. And at last came a faint strain of harmony: sweet, piercing, almost angelic; and after long, long silence I heard footsteps. A priest appeared with two priestesses who came to my side and gripped me first by the right arm, then by the left. I still lay as one dead until, after a short interval of unearthly quiet, the High Priest himself came and laid his right hand first on the brow, the thought-centre, then on the throat, the speech-centre, then on the heart, centre of love. With this threefold touch and sign I was able to stir, very slowly, and I opened my eyes on a radiant light that shone from a blue plaque of the sacred luminous stone at the far end of the cave. At first, when the priest raised and led me towards the plaque its brilliance confused me. Bright and polished, it acted as a mirror, reflecting not only my appearance but my inner self, my habitual thoughts and natural weaknesses. But it revealed as well the strength that could be mine if I clung steadfastly to the Light within. It showed not only my thought-and-feeling life but what lay deep in my heart, potentialities that could well into manifestation from the divine self in everyone.

I was urged to look deeper into the magic mirror and I saw possibilities that seemed infinite. As I stood amazed, an even more brilliant shaft of light was projected from above, a rod of light and power that came steadily to rest first on my head, then on my throat, and at last it rested and remained over my heart. The High Priest spoke words that sounded like rich chords of music from a heart charged with love and wisdom:

'My daughter, as your soul goes on its long journey through boundless life it will henceforth remain in the magic power of this light. For there is that in your heart which attracts it. Keep your heart clean and the magic of the gods will never fail. You are but a fragment, an atom, in God's universe, and this you will always remain. Power over life and death rests with God alone. No human is great. All you think you have is not yours but a part of God. No-one can rob God of divine power, but God destroys you when you set yourself to destroy God.

'Be at peace with life. Give all you work for to God. Love your neighbour as yourself and continue on the spiral path that will take you safely back to your Father–Mother. You will reap happiness and you will reap pain; but these experiences are seeds scattered on earth, and spiritual food will grow from them, sustenance for earth's children. The seed-joys and seed-pains men and women have to sow grow into the bread of life, food that nourishes human souls. The mystery of life lies in this. Ploughing and reaping, tilling the soil of earth-life, you shall live by the sweat of the brow until the fruit-bearing tree comes to perfection. Even so, we return to earth again and again to labour there, and return to heaven for refreshment, until God's will is done on earth as it is done in heaven.'

I still hear these words.

Then strange visions awoke in me. Just as To-waan had seen when he stood with the Master on the mountain, so now I too saw into past and future. Centuries unrolled, so that I saw not only my brief life with the Mayas but a vista of lives going far into the future in lands separated from this by half a world. I looked over the seas to a land of pyramids and temples where a dark-skinned people lived beside a great and placid river. I saw myself as a priestess there and the centuries rolled on, bringing to the etheric screen another life lived in China; and a life among people with white skins on a northern island. An outline of work to be done there was drawn with bold strokes. Even in this far future, I saw my beloved Hah-Wah-Tah still close to me and I knew that his strong love would survive many a death and parting, linking us through the centuries. I knew he was near me. Swaying, fainting, I called his name. A quick step and his arms were round me. He carried me to a prepared couch and gave me food and wine.

Minesta, the Mayan girl, had passed the third degree of initiation.

Chapter 6

The Wisdom of Hah-Wah-Tah

DURING early manhood, Hah-Wah-Tah went through the prescribed tests and gained illumination for mind and heart. He spent many months on the mountain with the Brothers of the Land of Light and they taught him the art of healing by colour rays drawn from the Sun and transmitted to the sick. They taught him as well how to withdraw from the dense body and go to the land of spirits, how to cross the great ravines in the mountains by levitation, and how to help those who were sick in mind. As time passed, To-waan and I learned how to make use of some of these magic powers and we grew to maturity in this simple, childlike community, taught by Chief Hah-Wah-Tah how to rule with love, how to live in peace with all human and animal life.

The Mayas never slew any creature wantonly. If it became necessary to kill for food they would do so, first thanking their brother the animal whose life they were compelled to take, for its sacrifice and for the gift of its flesh. A spirit of brotherhood, cheerfulness, kindliness and service pervaded the communal life, a spirit taught them by word and in deed by Hah-Wah-Tah. We all shared alike. No-one dreamt of taking more than another, for each recognized the other's needs.

Hah-Wah-Tah was wise in head and heart, with deep spiritual intelligence, for all he knew came from the illumination of his soul by God's light. He saw that the only possible basis for true law and just government was brotherhood: simple kindliness practised and lived. He knew that if brotherhood was established, peace must follow, with progress in arts and sciences, well-being in body, soul and spirit. And indeed the law of brotherhood, recognition of the equal needs and rights of all people, proved effective for the settlement of any problems that might arise in the affairs of our people.

On the first of each lunar month, the day of the new moon, Hah-Wah-Tah would attend his Court of Justice. This was held in a stone building, rather like a large summerhouse, where flowering vines grew up the stone pillars and over the dome they supported. The interior consisted of a fairly large assembly hall with a low wall that divided the court from the gardens, and an inner council chamber at the far end of the entrance-hall with an opening like a window that gave a wide view of the river and mountains on the horizon. Here, seated on a seat cut whole from the trunk of a great tree and shaped into a daïs or throne, its back carved in the figure of a plumed eagle and surrounded by grapes and wheat, Chief Hah-Wah-Tah listened with grave patience to the questions and problems his people and the younger chieftains submitted to him. Some came from over the mountains, others from villages near and far down the great river. Most were simple, primitive, kindly; yet a few harboured the seeds of doubt, fear and greed, the beginnings of discontent and strife.

A young chieftain named Armoric arrived one day to ask what he was to do in the event of a poor harvest that threatened his people with famine. His own lands were producing insufficient food, the chief of a neighbouring tribe refused to lend acreage except at an exorbitant price. Should he pay or should he take land by force of arms from his neighbour, knowing that he and his people could win and confiscate what they needed? If Armoric acceded to his brother-chieftain's demands he would probably impoverish his own people and make them go hungry pending a better harvest. He claimed every moral right on his side; the other man's attitude was harsh and wrong. He could fight and probably win. What should he do?

Hah-Wah-Tah listened intently and sat for a long while with eyes closed as if he consulted with those who were invisible.

He asked that the other chieftain be sent for, who having made obeisance before the Father of his people, debated nothing of his case and sought to justify it, pleading poverty and the need to accumulate ample stores against possible adversity. His own people's rights, he said, came before those of Armoric's tribe: if anyone suffered it should be they. Then he grew angry and incoherent under the gaze of those wise eyes that saw so deep into the heart, and at length fell silent.

Hah-Wah-Tah spoke gently as befits one who though in authority is kindly withal; yet there was weight, power, in every word and no word failed of its mark. 'The one who puts him-or-herself first, or the welfare of family or tribe before the common good, dies the slow death', he said. 'First, zest dies in the heart though no-one knows it, for the voice of conscience that should be a wise counsellor, becomes a canker. No longer is there any pleasure in living, and days are cloudy, heavy. The body becomes diseased; and death, instead of being mellow and kind, comes like a tyrant who brings cruel suffering. The unjust person cannot evade this. Nor will possessions remain, for the spirits of earth, air, water and flame, seeing one who truly deserves the slow death, will refuse their help. Crops will fail and storms will blast his or her property. Floods will drown cattle and sheep. Irresistible fire will devour the human substance. And the hereafter waits.'

Hah-Wah-Tah turned to Armoric. 'You have heard. If this

man chooses the way that leads to the slow death do not hate him, but rather pity him with all your heart, for he will need it. Harbour neither resentment nor bitterness. Cleanse yourself of these and the spirits of earth and air, water and flame will serve you in such manner that your crops will grow more plentiful and you will be rich in blessing. Hate the oppressor in your heart and you too will die the slow death. Suffer injustice with forgiveness and all will be well with you.'

Hah-Wah-Tah pleaded with the two chieftains. 'Brothers of my heart, will you not meet one another? I who am Hah-Wah-Tah would touch you with the hand of love, hold you together in brotherhood. My heart is sore because of your enmity. Take each other by the hand and go back to your place, asking the Great White Spirit to show you the way of blessing.'

Hearing this, the two went their way, hand in hand, like children that are sorry.

*

Presently a man and a woman were brought before the Chief for stealing the precious possessions of a former employer who had fallen sick through the loss. But when the accuser was questioned as to what had been stolen he declared that it wasn't gold or precious stones or good food, but these two had spoken untruthfully and evilly against him, with the result that many who had thought of him well and kindly now despised him. He had been robbed of a good reputation. How could he recover what their vicious tongues had taken so wantonly?

After deep thought, Hah-Wah-Tah said to the slandered man, 'There is no need to defend virtue. No-one can rob another of what has become an integral part of the soul. It is impossible to uproot goodness and purity from the heart. Vicious, empty and foolish words are like dust driven by the winds into nothingness, but with every cruel and unjust accusation or criticism, the shadow in the heart of the one that utters them grows darker and denser. Therefore it is your duty to inspire confidence in these two and to help them. If you can forgive and forget they will learn respect. They have caused you suffering, but there is a deeper scar in their hearts. Can you not pity them?'

. The man and the woman hung their heads when they heard the wisdom of the gods spoken so simply through the lips of their Chief. Their tongues had been vicious, wanton and cruel: they were deeply stained. And now they had seen truth in Hah-Wah-Tah's eyes and heard it in his words; they suffered the shame of their unworthiness. Needing no other punishment, they knelt with bowed heads and after a silence in which all three prayed to their God. Hah-Wah-Tah blessed each one, saying, 'Go in peace. Vow to keep henceforward the law of the brotherhood of the spirit'. The one who had fallen sick through fear lest his good name be lost went home to get on with his work, thinking with pity of the worse ill those two had brought on themselves. After a while pity showed him likeable and worthy traits in them, and forgiving them he grew well in body and in mind.

*

One day a young woman, Moo by name, was brought in by the people of her village. She was slim, graceful, gentle; and she was charged with violation of the law of sex they held sacred.

There was silence in Hah-Wah-Tah's council chamber while an older woman, with accusing finger, poured out a stream of words describing Moo's depravity. Downcast, motionless, the culprit stood as if she awaited deserved punishment. Hah-Wah-Tah in his chair of justice listened. Then, commanding silence, he asked Moo what she most wanted in life. Sadly, with drooping head she replied, 'I long above all to love truly and be loved, to hold my baby to my breast. But alas I have no husband, and my lover has been sent away from me to a village far down the river. I am unhappy and lonely'. Further questions brought out the fact that the older woman, the accuser, was the mother of Moo's lover and had herself parted them, hoping she could prevent her son marrying the girl by long separation.

Hah-Wah-Tah addressed her. 'There are sins of the mind far worse than those of the body. One can sin through greed of possession and by sinning lose all. The love your son once bore you now turns to dislike and fear. Do you not know that you are despoiled and bereft? Already widowed, you will soon be childless too, for your son's love has died. Contrast your sin with this child's. She has fallen through love, through her body's craving for the child you deny her, for the natural, rightful love of husband and wife. Woman, your sin is the more grievous, for you have driven this child to sin. Most grievous it is that you have made yourself accuser and judge of Moo who is hungry with mother-hunger for love and her child.'

Hah-Wah-Tah turned to the girl and said, 'My daughter, you have sinned. Yet who among us accuses you?'. No-one spoke. He continued, 'No man or woman accuses you save one. Your sins are forgiven because you loved. I give this woman into your hands. You shall pronounce judgment, Moo, and as you pronounce it shall be done'.

The girl came slowly forward and knelt before Hah-Wah-Tah. Some influence seemed to pass from him to her; some interchange of thought. She rose, sure of herself, bowed thrice and crossed to her accuser. For a moment the two gazed at each other, then fell into each other's arms. We watched while mother-and-daughter-to-be passed from shadow to sunlight with clasped hands.

Chapter 7

Minesta and the Master

FOR MANY months after the ordeal of initiation, I lived quietly at home, regaining physical strength and wellbeing. I was aware of increased power within myself and I realized gradually that it would be mine for ever. But I knew also that it waited for the years to come for its full unfoldment.

One day Hah-Wah-Tah and To-waan came to me with joy in their faces, saying, 'The Master has sent for us. We are to go to the Temple high up in the mountains, where he will await us'.

After careful preparation we embarked and paddled for two days up a stream that in time became so narrow that we had to abandon our canoe. From then on our journey became more arduous, until we came at length to the foot of a great waterfall with precipitous cliffs towering over it. Experienced as I was in mountain climbing the prospect appalled me; nevertheless, I set myself to the task and as the hours passed scaled dizzy heights and hung breathlessly to some niche that overlooked dreadful depths. But a power not myself sustained me, calling me on and up, while Hah-Wah-Tah and To-waan helped me every foot of the climb and at last, spent and breathless, we reached the plateau. Now I could see the ring of great pine trees at a short distance and, secluded among them, the temple of the Brotherhood of the White Light.

A hush, a sense of peace in the air, conveyed the impression that we stood on holy ground. We walked slowly, expectantly, towards the entrance of a stone building of remarkable design and workmanship, so geometrically perfect and symmetrical, so harmoniously situated among the trees, as to make a lasting impression in our memories. As we approached a man stepped from among the pines and came to us. I had long dreamt of this meeting! I was awed, almost afraid.

For who and what was this man, so noble in white robe embroidered with gold, wearing a white plumed headdress that resembled a great crown? As he drew near, I saw a gentleness of expression, a simplicity of demeanour, even a humility, surpassing anything I had imagined. There was that in his eyes, which showed me he already understood everything about me. But I need have felt no fear: his greeting was as natural as that of a loved parent. Something in his voice seemed to warm and pervade my heart; a light in his eyes illumined my very soul. I knelt at his feet, and he touched my head, blessing me.

After a silent interval, Hah-Wah-Tah and To-waan were blessed in turn; then all three of us followed the Master to the Temple. Here I was greeted by one of the priestesses who had been present at my initiation and had come here to rest. My father and To-waan were welcomed by priests, and we were led to rooms where everything was provided for our comfort after the long and difficult climb. Then, refreshed with the food and drink each found waiting in the apartment, we slept.

When the sun's first rays touched me I awoke, feeling no ill-effects from my journey, and sprang from my bed full of fresh, young life, to find that a new white robe of the Order had been put ready. I bathed and robed. While waiting for the expected summons I filled the time looking through the open window, whence I saw a magnificent panorama of mountains

and valleys across the pines. I marvelled and thought of the
potentialities in human kind, who have such a lovely world in
which to live and evolve.

While I was meditating on these things, the summons
came for me to join my father and brother in the shrine at the
heart of the temple. The chamber to which we were led was
circular and windowless, the walls softly luminous as if the stone
itself radiated light. A powerful beam shone from the domed
roof on the altar at the centre, a double cube of translucent
blue stone. A lamp, similar to those found later in Egyptian
tombs, was alight on it. This was the sacred lamp and flame of
the White Light that came from the doomed land of Atlantis
and which was kept burning throughout its ocean voyage and
journey up the great river until it reached its prepared resting
place in the shrine here on the mountain. It burned luminous
and pure, seeming to illuminate and reveal not so much the
form and features of those gathered round it as their hearts
and thoughts. Its ray was searching indeed, disclosing the finest
characteristic of soul each brother and sister could give to the
service of the Brotherhood.

The Master joined us and we four seated ourselves round
the altar in meditation. Celestial peace stole into our hearts
and made us, as it were, one soul. The Master spoke. 'My
brethren, you have travelled far, facing severe tests of courage
and endurance. We followed you in thought every step of your
way and sent you all the aid we could. You have been brought
here for a purpose. It is well that you should see from within
this temple what service can be given human kind. It is well
that you should know it, for the knowledge will enter your heart
and dwell there not only through this life but through lives on
earth when you will make good use of it. May it always be your

choice to follow the white magic, which means selflessness in service to further human kind's spiritual evolution. Always beware of black magic, the self-seeking and love of the power that gives domination over others.'

There was a pause. These quietly-spoken words had a strength in them that went deep into our consciousness, as if we listened to some profound harmony, some unfading truth.

The Master continued: 'Our work and mission throughout the centuries, for we ourselves are no longer subject to death, is to lighten the ignorance if human beings, to soften and assuage their angers and hates. We send light not so much to people's minds as to their souls. We do not persuade them to this course or that; we send them light and inspiration. They are free to accept or reject it, for free will is their right. But we continue to pour out the light of God, concentrating especially on those with authority over others and with responsibility for their lives. We try to inspire them that they may follow ways of brotherhood and peace.'

Again there was a pause while the power and light of heaven gathered in the shrine. Then the gentle voice went on: 'We may not try to change a person's destiny, for the divine law ordains that all must reap what they sow. But when light enters a person's heart, good will be sown instead of evil; and in time good, will overcome evil and absorb it. Our present task is to prepare for the coming to earth of the Son of God, who is the true light of human kind. He will be called Redeemer. We look forward over the centuries and we see a symbol of supreme sacrifice on a hill in an eastern land. A cross of light hangs in the dark sky of materialism, but one day all men and women will make their way to it and yield their small selves to their Creator, to their God-self. They will recognize their birthright and claim it. They will earn the title of being called son or daughter of God.'

In the silence that followed my heart filled with joy and sorrow. Who is this mighty one, I asked myself, this Son of God, who will prove greater even than the one who is speaking to us?

The voice resumed: 'We may not save nations from their destiny if greed, arrogance and selfishness have enslaved their minds. They must suffer a just retribution for it—this is the law. But if our love and service can help them to transmute their sin, then let us not fail or weary in sending love out to them as a beam of light, that it may awaken and stimulate the true life that lies asleep in their souls. Let us join hands, my brethren, and send out a ray of the thought-power of love and light'.

Hah-Wah-Tah grasped my right hand, To-waan my left. The spiritual power in the shrine was drawn into the human circle, a pulsing, radiant presence, a flaming torrent. We became the medium through which the power of spiritual hosts and angelic beings was directed on those for whom the cosmic rays were intended. The Master spoke and at each word—I guessed it was the name of some king or ruler of a nation, across the seas perhaps—there shone out from the temple a ray of light. My vision was so clear I could see where it went, on whom it rested, whether it entered the heart or was rejected. It went to humble men and women, to teachers and sages; or to succour men or women in trouble or bereavement. It went to kings and emperors, political leaders and persons in authority. It would envelop and rest on some soul in a passion of fear or hatred; it would seek out the people of some nation stricken with war or pestilence. Some were open to it; others closed themselves and the shaft of Light was turned ignorantly aside.

Yet the light was sent out to the good and the evil, with prayer and compassion, day by day, year by year, unremittingly.

*

Next day, rested and restored, we turned homeward; but the Master blessed us again before we left and spoke to each secret words that we hid in our hearts. These words became jewels, to be cherished and kept ever-shining.

I was never summoned to climb the heights again, nor to see the Master; but I often felt his thoughts closely about me or as a warmth and strength welling up in my heart. Some day, I knew, perhaps never again in my life as Minesta, perhaps not for many a long life to come, I should see him, I should hear again that tranquil voice, look into those eyes so bright with the Light of God.

Chapter 8

The Passing of Hah-Wah-Tah

A MESSAGE came one day to Hah-Wah-Tah, the message by the messenger no-one can disobey; but as he was now of great age it was not unexpected. He was told he must leave his people and travel far to the west, to the land of the hereafter where dwelt Amaru.

Death seemed as natural as birth to the Indians. They did not fear it, nor mourn any loss, for they knew it was temporary; thus bereavement left them neither embittered nor resentful. So when the time came, To-waan and I helped with tranquil minds and loving hearts to array the old Chief in his white ceremonial cloak. He said farewell and with his staff in his hand, the jewelled circlet on his brow, turned his face from the valley towards the high mountains, raised his right hand in blessing to all his children and bade us remember the gods' teaching, that 'where love once abides it remains, even through eternity'.

'Although I go far away,' he said, 'we are forever united in spirit. We shall meet again, for this is according to the Law'. Then he went on up the mountain, by the path that led to the dwelling of the White Brothers almost on its crest.

As he climbed, dusk gave place to a haze of golden light on the horizon. Hah-Wah-Tah was received by the Brothers who bade him enter and rest. They led him to a ledge that overlooked a valley down whose bed a great river flowed.

Here he lay down to sleep, deeply to sleep. Nor did he wake until dawn, the dawn of a new life; and the friends of his spirit whom he had loved long ago came to him. They came with spirits of woodland bird and forest animal that had given him companionship and affection, spirits of pine and birch, salamanders from the campfires that had warmed him, and cooked his food. Spirits of air that had sung to him in wind among trees, fairy sprites, water-people from the streams that had bathed him and quenched his thirst. All these attended his awakening in the spirit land and, dearest of all, the brethren and parents who awaited him there. Thus he passed from mortal death to unending life.

When To-waan and I had fulfilled our life's purpose, we too received our message. Memories of life in the land beyond the grave have dimmed, yet I recall how Hah-Wah-Tah came to me, put his arms round me and held me. We went all three together into a land of light and beauty such as I had dreamt of but never seen; a land of kindness where many friends of ours lived; a land where my soul was caught up in a mist of light, itself light and joy.

We lived there together while our earth-lives faded out of memory and tranquillity stole our burdens away. And Hah-Wah-Tah was still our teacher. He would tell To-waan and me about our future. 'The soul may not live forever in bliss', he said. 'Even here, life calls … it is a challenge, not an everlasting beatitude. Would you not learn more about the heaven worlds? Beyond this home of ours in the land of light are brighter and yet more beautiful spheres, height on height reaching ever nearer to God. Would you climb towards God as we climbed those heights to the Master? It means effort, suffering; but you wouldn't choose to rest even here for ever and ever?'.

'Tell me where I must go and what I must do', I answered.

'You must return, Minesta. You must be reborn to an earth-life. You must again know labour and sorrow, taste earthly joy and learn to suffer. Not once only but many times does the soul take up what it has left undone, try to learn what it left unlearnt, right wrongs it committed, do good to those it hated, forgive where it once harboured revenge.'

'I am ready, dear Hah-Wah-Tah. If you are near me.'

'Life must be taken up where it was laid down', he answered. 'The soul will meet those it once loved. It will be helped by those it helped, suffer at the hands of those it wronged. We two could never be parted even if we wished. But this is a decision only you can take, for none need leave heaven until the heart desires it. You may remain in tranquillity while the centuries pass ... but even here we have an inner as well as an outer self, and the inner self knows when it is evading the law of being'.

We found ourselves on a mountain of vision. Before us the world fell away into unimaginable depths and clouds swirled at the mountain's feet. 'Listen', said Hah-Wah-Tah. 'Listen with all your heart.'

I stood gazing down. I saw myself again as the girl Minesta sitting beside a stream, watching the little people. I saw the pine-ringed temple on the heights of the Andes. I saw the three of us climbing to the crest where we met the Master and felt again the thrill and warmth of his blessing. This and much else I remembered and earth-life cried out to me, cried out in sadness. For men and women had grown cold. Tides of cruelty swept over the nations. Fatherless children, widowed mothers, wailed and their cry reached heaven. I saw men riding to war.

I turned to my father in tears.

'You have heard', he said. 'The world cries to you, with the language of grief. It is for you to choose.'

'My father!' I cried. 'I have heard…. I still hear. I must go. I must go. Show me the way, my father, and keep close to me, for already my heart is fearful'.

PART II

THE LIGHT IN EGYPT

Foreword to Part II

AFTER the memories of a Mayan incarnation were completed I lived a busy life, working every day as an instrument for those in the land of light who wished to communicate. Because of the teaching White Eagle brought, I spent my time engaged in work healing, comfort and inspiration to the hundreds who sought White Eagle's help. And then, to my surprise, another window was opened and I looked into a life spent in Egypt.

I felt that what I saw must be recorded, but now I found it impossible to take my attention from the re-living of this Egyptian life and use my pen. However, it so happened that at this very time a friend came with an offer of help so that I was able to concentrate. We met at appointed times and when she had tucked me down with a hot-water bottle on a couch, she opened her notebook to record in shorthand all I was able to repeat of my new experience. It was remarkable that each time we met I was able to take up the narrative exactly where I had left it, without reference to the notes of the previous session. This procedure has obvious advantages, but it is perhaps less controlled, less conscious, more liable to inadvertent confusion of times and places. I cannot therefore be certain when and where the events recorded took place, indeed I think it possible that there may be a fusion of the memories of two different lives in Egypt, in which the same work was continued.

These memories came to me soon after the Second World War but they had a sequel in 1964 when a friend went to Egypt. During her tour she visited the Cairo Museum and was amazed to see brilliantly-painted statues of Nofret and Ra-Hotep, her husband. They were found in 1871 by Daninos in a tomb at Meidum, near Cairo and Memphis. A remarkable thing about the figure of Nofret, who is named in this book as Ra-min-ati's mother, is the resemblance to the description of Ra-min-ati in these pages. 'She is wearing,' the guidebook says, 'a close-fitting white garment that reveals the outline of her body. On her tufted wig is a band adorned with a floral pattern. Round her neck the Lady Nofret wears the larger necklace, the 'wesekh'. This consists of rows of different colours. When we look at her face we can note the gentle, candid expression and, even more, the calm manifest in her restrained poise.' Both statues show the right hand placed on the heart centre.

It may be asked why Nofret, who was Ra-min-ati's mother in my recollections, is named in the Museum as Ra-Hotep's contemporary and wife. It is suggested that Nofret, meaning 'the Beautiful', was also Ra-min-ati's name, but she was not called by it to avoid confusion with her mother.

On April 14th, 1964, White Eagle said, 'We would just like to say how amused we were to see one of our sisters looking at an image in Egypt. Had she known, she could have seen the one who is called Is-ra. We were there. Tell your friend that we guided her on her Egyptian holiday. We wanted her to make the link there and see Nofret'.

Near the statues of Nofret and Ra-Hotep stands one of the nobleman Ti, who was high priest as well as architect, vizier and sole companion to Pharaoh, and two of the high priest Ra-nefer. As to which of these is Is-ra, we have no clear indication although opinion leans towards Ti.

I must add that when I wrote this book I had no Egyptology to speak of. I was ignorant of Egyptian history, had never seen the Pyramids or the Nile and had read no books on the subject. I know now the Egyptian beliefs were infinitely complex and went through many changes during the thousands of years of the Egyptian civilization; the versions given out by the sages varied as time went on according to the requirements of a given period. I am aware too that much of recorded Egyptian history is itself a kind of symbolism, expressive of an inner development. The published account of experiences recollected in trance may therefore perhaps be described as para-historical. But it sets forth an unalterable truth. The reader will notice the linking of the Mayan and Egyptian incarnations and meet the Master I have come to know as White Eagle, who was Hah-Wah-Tah, Is-ra and Hiawatha. Behind him was, and is, another, yet greater.

Chapter 9

Ra-Min-Ati

WHITE Eagle and I were in the cave of the White Cross, resting and meditating. The lake glistened and shimmered in the sun and a scent of pines rose sweet as incense. I was once again in touch with the world of spirit—a timeless, magic world. All the lives I had lived were mine to recall: a touch of the knob, as if I were a radio receiver, and I could tune in to scenes of the past, to heights and depths of the soul's experience.

I saw myself as Ra-min-ati, priestess in the temple of Ra, trained and initiated in the mysteries. White Eagle was Is-ra, chief priest and counsellor to Pharaoh. I watched the unfolding story of the girl Ra-min-ati as one might watch a motion-picture; but instead of a series of photographs on celluloid I saw the record of a life as it had been lived and impressed on earth's etheric substance. I saw that when the time for Ra-min-ati's return to earth drew near, preparations were made as for one who is about to undertake a journey that will entail residence in a distant land. She was shown the man and the woman who were to provide her with a body and was drawn into harmony with her parents-to-be. For a time before birth she lived in a magical world, a state of dream-consciousness, in a home that was, as she understood it a perfect expression in form, colour and harmony of God's love. Early on, her future parents were brought in their dreams to visit her. At such times she was among fairies and angels who seemed to be spinning silver, gold and many-coloured gossamer threads between herself and the parents, and at last she felt as it were tied to them and her new home on earth. Then she became unconscious and slept.

Ra-min-ati was born when her parents were young. Her name, given her because she was born at daybreak, had been agreed with the high priest and astrologer Is-ra, who predicted the moment. Moreover he told her mother, Nofret, that he had long awaited her arrival. 'Your daughter-to-be was once my own', he said, 'so I await her rebirth in great happiness'.

Nofret, sister to the reigning Pharaoh, was considered a woman of great beauty. She was small and dainty, with olive skin and brown eyes, and straight black hair that reached nearly to her shoulders. She wore it parted in the middle and kept it in place with an embroidered gold band. A white linen gown embroidered with blue and sun-colours, a bright clear lacquer red predominant, particularly enhanced her beauty. In her early teens she married Tahuti, a priest in the temple of Ra (for Egyptian priests married, had families and spacious homes). She was a wise mother, gentle in speech, kind and thoughtful; but she insisted on obedience from her children and taught them courtesy. She would spend many hours playing with them and answering their questions.

Tahuti was regarded by his family and many others as a friend and counsellor who by strength of character, sympathy and humour commanded respect. His eyes, the poise and carriage of his tall, lissom body, expressed power and insight. He was descended from an early Mayan priest, and had the features of an American Indian, aquiline nose, deep-set eyes, a penetrating gaze, straight forehead, and firm yet mobile lips.

They lived in a spacious, square house of white stone on

the raised bank of the Nile, commanding a view of the river. It was a type of house that officials and priests built for themselves, but they kept it for one generation only. Each family owned its house, and when a couple married they made a fresh home, a custom that has much to recommend it, because, as it was believed, the thought-forms of earlier residents may cling to an old house and the effect is not always good for their successors. There were many similar houses, standing above the high-water level to prevent their being flooded when the Nile rose. Channels were cut at intervals along the riverbank to carry water into the farmlands and irrigate gardens, which were always well planned and cultivated. The Nile waters were also used to provide power for the construction of temples and public buildings. Is-ra said that similar, magical power was used to build pyramids and drive aircraft in Atlantis and Mu.

Ra-min-ati's childhood was full of joy. The Egyptians were Sun-people who worshipped not only the visible orb that gave light and life but also the spirit in the physical manifestation. Beauty, harmony, laughter—these were the keynotes of their colourful lives, for they believed that Ra gave them the gifts of this rich land to use for their pleasure. Ra-min-ati used to sit on a shaded balcony watching the pageantry of decorated state barges that glided up and down the Nile. Tahuti owned as well, or rather leased from the state, many acres of farmland. His ornamental garden was well designed with lawns, flowerbeds and artificial lakes and streams; it was surrounded by vineyards, orchards and fields of corn or vegetables. This society was communal. Religion, education and government, agriculture, poetry and music, architecture and sculpture, art and science were all founded on spiritual experience, based on principles derived from a conception of the one, supreme

Source of life, that manifested in its essential duality through the male principle Ra and the female principle in several aspects, of which Isis was one. The children were taught service to the community, a conception of social and religious behaviour handed on age after age in one land or another by priests of the House of Light. The rites and customs of those times were similar to those of the Mayas.

When, at seven years old, children were sent to a communal school, they were already used to putting the community before themselves. Early education was devised to open the way for psychic development through the natural, full and correct use of the five senses, so that the soul-body was helped in its growth. Even tiny children were encouraged to be observant. Thus, Ra-min-ati was early instructed in exercises that taught her to make use of her eyes, watching the cloud-shapes, noting the direction of the wind, spotting birds on the wing, noting the unfoldment of buds and formation of fruit. This was a favourite game, played in field or garden, that we called 'I spy'.

Another game was listening to the wind, birdsong, insect or animal noises, the oars and paddles of barges on the river, which so quickened their sense of hearing that children grew extremely sensitive sometimes even to what is normally beyond the limit of hearing, such as music of fairy pipes or fairy songs. To develop their sense of touch, children played with sand and learnt to mould clay into the form of birds and animals. They made bricks and sun-baked them, colouring them with bright water-dyes. They built models of houses, workshops and temples. Teachers, and sometimes one or both parents, would join in the games. Ra-min-ati's father invented the game of guessing plant, tree or flower by its perfume. The children were blindfolded and led within a yard of some bush or tree; then, guided by their sense of smell, they would name it. If they did so correctly, their eyes were freed; if not, they had to try the scent of one plant after another until they found the right answer. In time, they could actually smell the aura of anyone who approached, and could guess who it might be.

Ra-min-ati bathed daily with her brothers and sisters in a pool near the house. They liked to feel air and water on their bodies as they splashed and played water-games with brightly coloured balls. Food was simple and pure, consisting chiefly of fruits, nuts, vegetables both cooked and raw, lentils, rice, corn, wheat meal, and sometimes the flesh of ox or wild duck. They drank goat's milk, wine and unfermented fruit-juices, especially orange-juice. Ra-min-ati learnt early to distinguish the flavour of fruit, vegetable, herb or nut and to draw the maximum of taste and nourishment from them. This too helped to develop the subtler senses of the soul-body. Indeed, the children well understood that their senses were ports of entry, open not only to the sight, sound, taste, smell and touch of physical objects but to the etheric counterpart; they knew that the etheric system flashed knowledge through sensory experience to the mind. The aura is an emanation from the soul-body, a vibration produced by thought and emotion. By means of it, people can become aware of invisible life. The education of the senses was in fact designed to enhance awareness of normally invisible, impalpable, inaudible forms in the light-world, and Ra-min-ati was taught later how to look into it.

When Ra-min-ati was twelve years old, Nofret took her to the temple of Ra, where she was presented to Is-ra, the High Priest, to be prepared for service to the community. At this time she was a slim, brown-eyed girl with very dark hair parted in the centre and cut in a straight line at the neck. Her usual dress was a one-piece garment of fine white cloth, embroidered at neck, sleeves and hem with a many-coloured design of flowers or fruits, sometimes butterflies or birds. She wore a look of happiness; but when she was taken by some truth or mystery her expression changed to one of intensity and her eyes seemed to look beyond this world into secret things.

Chapter 10

The High Priest Is-Ra

IS-RA HAD trained Nofret regarding the things of this world and of the spirit. She told Ra-min-ati many of Is-ra's stories and showed the child how much the high priest was loved by his pupils through his understanding of youthful minds and hearts. So Ra-min-ati looked forward eagerly to her acceptance in the temple as Is-ra's pupil.

When the day came, she went with her mother on board a barge from the steps of their garden and glided along the stream to a square stone building called the Hall of Learning and Justice. By now, she had begun to feel nervous over her first meeting with a high priest who was also guardian of this awe-inspiring place. They disembarked and climbed massive steps that led to the centre of the building. On either side of the entrance stood columns of sandstone carved with the head of the sphinx. Crowning the arch, set in gold, which glittered in the morning sunlight, was the scarab, symbol of the Creator imprisoned in matter. The silence of the temple enfolded them as Nofret led her daughter into the main hall and towards the stone altar, where seven little oil lamps burned, set on a stand like a seven-branched candlestick. Behind and above the altar a winged disc blazed in gold. The power and solemnity of the place sank into Ra-min-ati's young mind.

After some time a tall figure came towards them. From whence he came, Ra-min-ati had no idea: a man clothed in white linen, girdled with a gold belt, wearing a crown of soft white feathers with a gold band in which seven jewels were set. At first she felt rather than saw his serene presence; then a hand rested on her head, turned her gaze upward to meet deep violet-blue eyes that looked at her with humour and kindliness, and at last she realized suddenly that this was someone very near and dear. When he spoke, calling her his daughter, she knew that at some time or other she had been, indeed still was, his child. She tried to remember their last meeting, but her mind revealed nothing. He read the thoughts that raced through her child-mind and smiled again, saying, 'You are puzzled, little one, but have patience. The mists will clear and you will see me not through a veil but face to face and you will know the joy of reunion'.

Strange words, but they fell peacefully into her heart and she was content to listen to, learn from, and obey the priest-teacher whom in youthful wholeheartedness she accepted.

There was now perfect understanding between them and he said no more. With a sign he dismissed Nofret, who bowed and withdrew, never turning her back on the altar with the winged sun, symbol of Ra, high over it. Is-ra then led Ra-min-ati through the temple, explaining the significance of pictures painted on the walls and the orientation of the halls, no doubt to make her feel happy and familiar with her surroundings. At length they climbed a stairway of white stone that led to a balcony over the entrance and to the main building, with views of the Nile flowing between richly-cultivated fields, orchards and gardens.

'Today,' said Is-ra as they stood there in sunlight, 'you have begun a new phase of your life and your feet are set on a path of ever-increasing happiness. Truth and knowledge are within and around you, waiting to be discovered and developed. By study and meditation on the life of Ra in and through the perfect law that governs human life, by seeking his will and obeying his commands, which are only to be heard in the deep silence of your heart, you will attain. Knowledge, truth, love, wisdom, power, these can only come to you when the stream of light and life flows steadily from Ra into your heart, which is your most inward sanctuary. Meet your Creator there at the beginning of each day. Ask His will, that your work may have good fruit. We shall meet daily, we two, and you will be instructed in the holy law and its application to the needs of material and spiritual life. Tomorrow morning I shall wait for you before the steps in the Hall of Learning. Until then you may walk as you will through temple and gardens and meet your new friends. May you receive the blessing of the Light into your heart.'

*

Some days later, the big temple doors slid open and Ra-min-ati followed Is-ra down a flight of steps into a garden of flowering trees and shrubs, then under a pergola of blossoming vines that led into a walled garden. The scent of the flowers and the tranquil atmosphere were conducive to meditation; indeed it was for this purpose that they had sought the garden on this particular day. Is-ra directed her to a seat in the eastern corner and took her left hand. Soon she was in deep meditation. With Is-ra beside her it was easy to lose the turmoil of thoughts that centre on physical life and revolve round it. The clamour and stress of the lower mind were stilled, the world looked different, for now the colours of flowers became more vivid and scents were sweeter, birdsong sounded more beautiful. Everything in the garden was etherealized; Ra-min-ati was looking into another world where fairies worked in the flowerbeds, gnomes and elves trotted about well-kept paths. The garden teemed with life that had been invisible, yet there was no sense of intrusion. All shared one life, all were companions in spirit, understanding and appreciating each other's thought and work.

The sight of this inner life in nature was not altogether novel or surprising to Ra-min-ati. She knew it resulted from a tuning-up of her inner self so that it responded to a quicker and more harmonious vibration. Later she realized that this was a first step and Is-ra was preparing her for further initiation into invisible worlds. A long time must have passed while they sat there in silence; but Ra-min-ati was now unconscious of time, although fully aware of what was happening on the inner planes. Then the garden faded and she found herself in a far country in time long ago, watching people at work in the fields, on the farmlands, building temples and great stone buildings. She knew the temples were being raised to the Sun-God. As in a swift-moving picture she saw pyramids take form by means of some cosmic force that was directed by the divine intelligence, a process in which the peasant workers were used by a power not their own to lift the huge blocks and guide them into place where the same force welded them together. Now the world looked to Ra-min-ati like an anthill and the tiny creatures on it, men and women, lived and worked only to obey an impersonal will.

At first she thought it cruel to make people work thus. Reading her thoughts, Is-ra said, 'This is only what you see on the surface of human life; but when you look with insight and true perspective you will see far more than a response to impersonal stimuli. You will see the nobility in human life as you have seen the real beauty of the flowers in this garden. Every urge, every aspiration towards true beauty and freedom is recorded in the cosmos; it sets instantly in motion exactly the power that is necessary to bring the soul what it needs. God's world isn't cruel, my child, but a school where the children are meant to be happy, where they should know joy in the daily experiences of life and love, in change, in decline and rebirth. Human sorrows, hardships—the toil and weariness of human life—come from want of wisdom, ignorance of spiritual reality. Come, I have more to show you.'

When Ra-min-ati felt sufficiently her daily self again, she rose. They passed through gates beyond the sanctuary walls and wandered for some time along the many pathways of the temple gardens. The sun was setting when they reached a small stone building, a miniature temple that was used as a private meditation-place. On one side a shrine was built into the wall, on the other stood a couch. There was nothing more. Resting on the couch, Ra-min-ati thought over her experience long and deeply.

*

Ra-min-ati spent many hours in the garden sanctuary, where Is-ra came every day to give instruction. He taught her to meditate, to go out of her body into the inner world and rise through the astral planes. He often sent her on special missions into the inner world, but at first she was only allowed to undertake them in her sleep-state.

As she and Is-ra walked through the gardens one morning, they met a woman carrying a basket of grapes. She made a picturesque figure as she went to the winepress, balancing the basket on her sleek, black head. The red and gold of her kilt and an orange kerchief intensified the dark brown of almond-shaped eyes set wide apart in an oval, olive-skinned face, but the lines between them told of a fight with pain. Ra-min-ati recognized her as the wife of one of the temple gardeners, and noted with compassion that she seemed to gaze into the future with fear, haunted by her thoughts. 'Good morning, Zara,' said Is-ra. 'You are at work early.'

Zara gave a shy smile and her glance rested enquiringly on Ra-min-ati, but she did not stop.

'Stay a moment', said Is-ra. 'This is Ra-min-ati. You will often meet in the gardens, so you must be friends'. The two smiled at each other and a bond of sympathy was established.

Later, Is-ra told Ra-min-ati that it was in Zara's karma that she would soon leave the physical body. 'Is she afraid?', Ra-min-ati asked.

'Very. And if nothing is done to help her she will be lost in mists that arise from her own fears.'

'Can I help her?'

'You can visit her in your astral body every night when she is asleep. She won't know you at first, because her soul will be wandering on one of the nearer astral planes. You must watch her and choose the moment when her soul-body lights up. It will be one night when some special kindness from a friend has made her happy. Take her then by the hand. Lead her very gently to a garden-sanctuary—there are many in the astral world. Sit there and talk about the beauty of the surroundings. Explain that she will go to just such a place after death. Soothe her mind, Ra-min-ati. Help her to overcome fear. It is her karma that causes her state, but at heart she is good and true. She has given her family and her friends loving service. Happiness awaits her in a delightful home, where she will be with friends of her earth-life. We mustn't let fear hinder her journey to that true home.'

'Will she see me while she sleeps?', Ra-min-ati asked.

'Not at first. She will hear your voice faintly. Every night when you fall asleep, will yourself to find her wandering, fearful spirit, and then with all your power project a ray of white light to her.'

'How can I do this?'

'By thinking and feeling love for her, love only. It will be visible as a beam of light. It will attract her attention and awaken her sooner or later in the astral world. Then she will see you and hear you. Try to win her confidence. She will remember nothing about her earth-life, knowing only the immediate present. Talk to her as to a new friend about lovely things such as the garden-sanctuary; then ask if she would like to come home with you and take fruit, cakes, wine.

'She will be glad to do this, and you will find yourselves at once in a sanctuary like this. First get her interested and absorbed in your garden. Then when the meeting ends and the call comes to you both to return to your sleeping bodies, ask her to meet you again in the same place. She won't know yet that she is merely asleep on earth, for while in one state of consciousness she will forget the other. For instance, when she wakes in the morning she won't even remember your meeting in dream, any more than she remembers at night when she's asleep anything of her life in the body.'

Is-ra paused a moment. 'Through patient companionship during the night', he continued presently, 'you will in the end be able to open her eyes and help her to see the life she is really living both sides of the veil. She will begin to notice that when she is with you she feels much the same as in her daily existence. She will know that she is still real: living, breathing, eating. You will always give her cakes, fruit and wine when she comes to your garden. Soon she will grow used to meeting other friends who will join you from time to time; and then, when all this is familiar to her, you will tell her the truth, that she is spirit, that her body lies asleep beside her husband in her home on earth. Yes, it will shock her at first, but you will gradually convince her that it is true.'

'How will she remember when she is back in her body that she has visited her astral home?', Ra-min-ati asked.

'Your task is to teach her how to awaken her brain to such memories. You will do this by visiting her in her sleep and focusing on her brain a beam of brilliant light that your powerful thoughts of love will create in the ether. Such thought is a creative life-force and miracles can be done with it. Love is both a physical force and an ethereal substance, a light. Very few men or women have discovered the secret. Few even guess what real love can do. When you have passed your tests and proved yourself steadfast, obedient, you will be taken to the halls of initiation and admitted to the sanctuary of the White Light, the Hall of the Star, where you will see many a secret unveiled. You will not only see, you will actually pass through the flame of pure love. But that time is not yet, my child. You have much to learn before you are ready for it. Every night from now on therefore you must find your charge and help her until she can pass through one of the major initiations.'

'A major initiation? I don't understand', said Ra-min-ati.

'Death is an initiation and Zara must be prepared for it. She must be made ready for death on earth and birth into the light of reality. You, Ra-min-ati, will earn the joy of seeing her happiness when she is at last freed from her sufferings. You will companion her in the heaven world for a time when this happens, for you have shared her pain and her sorrows in imagination and loved her.'

At first, Ra-min-ati found it difficult to do as she was told. Doubts and fears beset her, especially when she missed Is-ra's presence for several days. Alone, her mind was apt to wander; concentration and meditation seemed impossible. She persevered nevertheless through trial and failure, gradually gaining confidence until at last success was hers.

The work with Zara went on for many weeks. Night after night they met in the astral world, and Ra-min-ati talked about the soul's life and the satisfactions people find after death. She explained that when the body dies the soul goes to a land of light; that souls are not parted from those they love on earth, because they gain wider consciousness when released from the body. They also travel far more easily and may visit their friends. As soon as those living on earth fall asleep, they can move in the spirit-world as easily as those who have died. At length, Zara began to understand that she could never be parted from the husband she loved, for at any time during sleep he could meet her and they would be together in a home more beautiful than any they knew on earth. But some little time elapsed before Ra-min-ati could make her understand fully that she was indeed living in two worlds, or realize that when she had absorbed all she could learn in earth life her body would fall away, die, while her spirit would live on in this heaven.

Thus Zara was prepared for her passing; and when it happened, the transition meant no more to her than a falling asleep and awakening, an awakening in her new home, to rest. Afterwards Ra-min-ati taught her to return to earth, wait for her husband to sleep and lead his unconscious soul back home with her. There she would awaken him and answer his questions, where they were, why they were together when he had thought her dead. In this way Zara and Mengebet lived with one another in spirit and learnt to receive Ra's light.

Is-ra explained that this was the kind of work the Brothers would demand of her, to awaken light in those ready to advance on the inner planes.

Chapter 11

The Chapel of Memory

SOME weeks later, Is-ra and Ra-min-ati went to the shrine in the garden, where she lay down on the couch and the priest seated himself beside her. Almost at once she went so deep into meditation it was almost trance, and found herself in a temple of light.

Is-ra accompanied her. As they were crossing the floor of a great hall they were met by a figure similar to Is-ra, having the same nobility in his face. His eyes were violet-blue—full of power, wisdom and love—and his hair sun-colour. He was robed in white; a golden girdle gleamed round his waist, a violet cloak with jewelled clasp hung from his shoulders. But in spite of his magnificent appearance, Ra-min-ati saw he was humble and simple in himself; once more this was someone she knew intimately, though she could not remember where they had met. Instantly Is-ra answered her thought. 'It is good that your spirit recognizes your Master though centuries have passed since you saw him. When you kneel before the high altar to receive the blessing of Ra you will be given a fuller reply to the question that is in your mind.'

Ra-min-ati crossed the tessellated floor to an altar blazing with light like the sun's. Light streamed from columns that supported the roof and music sounded in every part of the building, while voices could be heard chanting far off. She knelt, waiting. Her heart centre seemed to open and expand so that she was

united with all life. For an ineffable moment she was part of
the cosmic life-force. The temple filled with an innumerable
throng, and she knew every soul among them; each was part of
herself, she herself part of them all. Harmony, peace and love
pervaded the hall as the Master intoned magical words: 'Love is
light. Let the light shine!'. Again there was music and chanting;
then the light that was already so brilliant grew in radiance so
that it seemed to impregnate every etheric and spiritual atom
before it waned, leaving a warm glow and peace.

When this was over the hall emptied and Ra-min-ati was
alone with her Master and Is-ra.

*

Around the main hall were smaller chapels, where those seeking to know their innermost self and learn their Master's will
could meditate and pray. Ra-min-ati was guided to one of
these and saw that 'The Chapel of Memory' was written over
it. The walls seemed to be made of an amethyst stone whose
glow filled the atmosphere with violet; but once she was in the
chapel they became transparent—so that, no longer enclosed,
she could look out on a life that seemed familiar. Her memory
of it awoke and she knew that in time long past it had been
customary to travel through the air in a ship not unlike a metal-
lic bird. Now in her vision she watched such a bird glide to a
station-platform high above ground on a tower. People emerged
from the airship's side and disappeared for a moment; then
they were to be seen in a funicular that took them down to the
street-level of a splendid and gracious city.

Ra-min-ati saw that the roads were wide, clean and bor-
dered with flowering shrubs and trees. The buildings, of pure
white stone, were designed in a 'square' style, with entrances,
steps and colonnades that reminded her of Egyptian temples.

As her vision roamed over the city she saw in the distance a range of snow-capped mountains, one of which stood out with greater clarity than the others, dominating them. The Master who was guiding her on this etheric journey said, 'You are seeing the holy mountain near the ancient capital of Atlantis. At its apex the temple of the White Magic stands. A colony of men and women who had been initiated in the mysteries lived there before the sea engulfed a great continent. Priests taught religion there and helped in the government of the land, their sole purpose to serve human kind through wisdom and justice, to formulate laws for the people's happiness and wellbeing, and to advance the spiritual evolution of the race.'

Ra-min-ati noticed that the base of this temple was in the form of a cube and the crown looked like four triangles meeting in a pyramid. The Master answered her thoughts. 'Sages who knew the mysteries left this ancient land and settled in sun-baked Egypt. They carried mysterious powers and taught the Egyptians to build temples and carve great stones as symbols of the Wisdom. The knowledge they had was brought to them from another planet in our system'.

Memories of this old, wondrous land with its holy mountain standing over the white city became vivid reality to Ra-min-ati. She saw herself walking beside a wide river that flowed through the city. She watched small sailing boats and large cargo boats with bright-hued sails passing upstream or down, for this was a nerve-centre of a great and highly-civilized race. Its people were mostly white-skinned with dark hair and soft brown eyes, although some had fair or red hair and blue or green-blue eyes like the people of Egypt. As this vision opened to her she began to understand some of the mystery of her own land and people and recognized in them descendants of these colourful, happy, laughter-loving children who lived in a western land in a golden age. Thus when the Master spoke again to her quickened consciousness she knew the truth in his words. Memories of the past were rekindled to vivid life and she felt the time had come for a wider expansion of consciousness than she had yet known.

*

There was a locked door in the wall of Ra-min-ati's private sanctuary in the temple garden. When Is-ra first took her there she asked where it led. 'When you are ready', he answered, 'I shall touch the secret spring and it will open. Then you will see that it bars the way through underground labyrinths to the Hall of the Sphinx and the Star Chamber beneath the Pyramid'.

'What is the meaning of the Sphinx?' she asked.

'It is a symbol of immemorial age, familiar to the people of lands that have now vanished. It signifies the eternal mystery of God in human kind, in all creation. It signifies also human victory over the lower, animal nature. It is for the candidate to find out the rest. All candidates for initiation into the White Brotherhood must first study the Sphinx's outer meaning. They will observe its construction and remark that it embodies their own potential qualities. They discipline themselves to be as silent in their wisdom as the Sphinx itself. They strive to attain the lion's strength and to grow an eagle's wings. They aspire to all the qualities that silent figure expresses. And a door between the Sphinx's paws admits the candidate into labyrinths that lead to the Hall of Initiation.'

Ra-min-ati listened intently while Is-ra continued. 'A pyramid symbolizes, first, the square base on which everyone's life must stand. Then, as the four triangular sides of the pyramid meet at the apex, so there must be exact correspondence between the four sides of the human nature—the physical, emotional, mental and spiritual components—before a true and perfect temple can be formed in the soul. Priests of the White Magic have always taught that men and women were created perfect sons and daughters of the Being, the Sun, we call Ra, in Ra's own image. They have taught that the radiant divinity, only spirit can know, Ra's pure bright light, is in every human being. They have further taught that a subtle essence shines in the rays of the physical sun, which affects earth as a mother who receives and nurtures the seeds of life. But this light exercises its magic most powerfully in the human soul; and in this lies the secret of happiness. Light is Ra's most precious gift to his children. Each must discover this in and for him- or herself.

'When the cube is opened out, it takes the form of a cross, perhaps the oldest of all symbols. The cross symbolizes creation, the creator innate and imprisoned in matter. Pyramid and cross then have fundamental significance.'

Much that had baffled Ra-min-ati was becoming plainer. Is-ra continued. 'The triangle symbolizes another cardinal truth—the trinity that is inherent in the Being of God, the will- and power- principle, the love- and wisdom-principle, and what proceeds from them—the principle of the light and God-consciousness in humanity. In manifestation, this trinity has many names—Osiris, Isis–Horus, for example. Thus the pyramid symbolizes an indestructible temple, a meaning, a reality, built on earth by Ra's perfected children. Few realize that it holds all the secrets of creation and exhibits the qualities that will bring each man and woman to final initiation in the celestial mysteries.'

Once more Is-ra paused, and then continued. 'Long ago

the Masters, instructed by the Sons of Ra, left Atlantis and settled in Egypt, where they established their religion and symbolizm and instructed the people in a system of government that was first introduced in Mu, a continent that has also disappeared. The pyramid holds all their secrets. It is oriented to the sun and the angle of the sun's rays on its apex has a significance you will come to understand, as all initiates do. But notice that on certain days of the year a shaft of light penetrates the recesses of these and other temples, as the light of Ra penetrates the human temple and dwells there.'

*

Ra-min-ati had now been a pupil of the high priest for seven years, during the last four of which she lived entirely within the precinct. 'Your training would be interrupted and made unnecessarily difficult', he explained, 'if you constantly paid visits in the outer world. While you are here you are protected from innumerable influences which would break into your meditations and your contacts with spiritual spheres.'

The two passed many hours in communion in the halls of learning beyond earth. 'This is the only true way to get knowledge of the Ancient Wisdom', said Is-ra, 'by which we mean knowledge of the cosmic laws, natural and spiritual, that govern human life. As the ages have passed, such knowledge has been lost in the selfishness and materialism that tend increasingly to swaddle and imprison the real self as mummy-wrappings swaddle the true form of a dead king. Until you penetrate the shrouding darkness that comes from worldly thoughts and habits you cannot understand or recapture the beauty with which the Lord Ra endowed you. You are being taught, Ra-min-ati, to see through the mists of illusion into the wisdom of past ages.'

Is-ra then took her to an antechamber west of the temple. Except for mirrors, the walls were bare of decoration, and as in the chapel of memory, rich amethyst-colour, a hue that seemed to Ra-min-ati to quicken her sight. Is-ra led her to a couch on which she at once fell into unconsciousness of the world about her and found herself in a country quite unlike Egypt. She knew she was again on the mountain heights of 'the land of the west', in a cave hewn in the rock, richly furnished with coloured rugs and carved furniture. A seat near the opening commanded a view across snow-capped peaks and a deep, pine-covered gorge lay in the foreground. A figure sat gazing out over this panorama.

It startled her somewhat to recognize this figure as herself, wearing a different dress. Then she heard a voice saying, 'It is good, Minesta, that you have returned to our Brotherhood. We will help you to remember the ways and customs of our people'.

The whole picture of her life in the Maya country grew vivid. She slipped in a flash from her Egyptian self into the Mayan Indian she had been. She saw again the peaceful valley with the quaintly-carved little houses of white stone reaching far up the mountainside, blue smoke curling against a background of giant pines, the broad, swift-flowing river. Another memory stirred and quickened. Once again she was sitting on a favourite log watching the nature-spirits at work and play among the rocks, plants, flowers and the tumbling waterfalls that cascaded over great boulders on the riverbanks. By her side a tall figure appeared and she recognized in the stalwart Indian her father, Hah-Wah-Tah: even as she saw the affection and humour in his eyes, she knew that Is-ra was the same beloved companion. Her mind flashed back to a temple on the mountain heights that towered above her old home. She remembered the gathering of White Brothers, the ceremony of calling down fire to light the heaps of dried sticks. She heard the high priest's voice call on the gods of the nature worlds. She felt simple kindliness pour from the peoples who were giving heart and soul to aid the priest in the ceremony that invoked the powers of nature, to direct the course of the wind-currents and in due time bring rain. She remembered how the priests called on the sun-spirits by whose aid the sun warmed, quickened and ripened the seeds, so that food would be assured. She re-lived these and many a happy scene that her Egyptian experience recognized as the worship of Osiris and Isis.

*

Now Ra-min-ati found herself in a temple of white stone in the company of white-robed priests. At their head, standing before a cubed altar of blue stone that looked like lapis lazuli, she saw the Master who long ages before laid his hand on her brow so that her eyes were opened and she foresaw her life in Egypt. And a young Indian chief stood beside her, her brother, and she remembered how they ruled the tribes together in Willomee. 'You have returned, Ra-min-ati', came the Master's voice, 'as you will return again and again to receive knowledge and wisdom from the White Brotherhood'.

Now the White Brothers were chanting Mayan words of power, and a star blazing with light and colour appeared in their midst. Once again she saw its rays projected over the world. She recalled the precepts of this most ancient Brotherhood, understanding the principles on which right and just government should be based, from which the fundamentals of right education and culture must derive. Now she could return and take up her life in Egypt with new knowledge and as time passed she would introduce the wisdom so wonderfully revealed in the land of sunshine.

Chapter 12

Ra-Hotep

DURING early manhood, Ra-Hotep lived in an outlying province, from which he would sometimes come to attend the ceremonies that were held in the great temple of Ra. Few of his friends would have regarded him as a religious man, although he was sometimes deeply stirred by the spiritual forces at work in the ceremonials. A sensitiveness to such powers, a potential spirituality, was to be discerned in his carriage, his well-balanced head, in deep-set, dark and unfathomable eyes that seemed to have caught and held some mystery of the desert; moreover, lips and chin suggested self-control and discipline, with a hint of obstinacy perhaps.

Some years before, Ra-Hotep had been appointed scribe to the king-priest, the ruling Pharaoh, and numbered many nobles and elders of the court among his friends, while his enemies were few. In youth he had enjoyed to the full the light-hearted gaiety common to Egyptians, but as he matured he tended to weary of this life and to interest himself in matters concerning the inner life. An urge to know more sometimes drove him to seek solitude and commune with the invisible forces of nature.

Like all Egyptian youths, he had served in Pharaoh's army in various distant garrisons, where he had acquired some excellent qualities and some not so excellent. Loneliness had taught him much, although now sometimes he feared being too much alone; but privation had to some extent hardened his character. This was largely protective armour against intrusion or ridicule.

Contact with others brought insight of their weaknesses and he suffered many a disappointment through placing his trust unwisely. In time this taught him to rely on no-one but himself; but at times he failed to satisfy the disciplinarian who resided in his own consciousness. His motto might have been, 'If you want a thing done properly, do it yourself'. But whereas he wished to lead an independent and self-sufficient life, he had yet to learn how impossible it is for a person to live happily in mental and spiritual isolation. As things were, Ra-Hotep preferred to call no-one his friend, nor yet anyone his enemy; but he was beginning to recognize that some people, possibly all, had something to teach him.

This philosophy was perhaps sound enough, if incomplete. He was emotionally unawakened. He had functioned nearly all his life on the mental plane, so that his spiritual potentialities were but partially developed. To quicken him and open his heart, he needed such an experience as the love of a man for a woman perhaps. Indeed, it is only human and natural love that can do this, love for a friend, for a child, for a spouse. The mind may accumulate a wealth of facts, but without development of his love-capacity, or—as the priests taught—an opening of the heart-centre, none can learn the secret of white magic; only through love can we learn to use mind-knowledge for the benefit and uplifting of human life. Until then, a man or woman is a theorist. Afterwards life is lived for itself.

Through some intense experience of love, and perhaps disappointment, of joy, and perhaps anguish, the miracle of transmutation from instinct to higher consciousness can be effected. The unenlightened, who live for pleasure, seeking to avoid pain, will have not only to retrace their steps but to readjust their ideas. As they awaken they will find that every experience is intensified, until in time they learn that there is no other way to climb the holy mountain but the way of aspiration and endeavour. Sweet, human love between man and woman, particularly when it is raised above selfish desire, can afford the soul a stepping-stone from the things of the world to the things of the spirit and raise it from earth to heaven.

Although self-reliance and self-confidence were his gods, Ra-Hotep often felt the need of companionship. He would never admit this to himself, thinking he preferred solitude, isolation, seeking no intimate friendships, planning, if he must know disappointment again, to take it himself alone. But during the Festival of the Finding of Osiris, held on the fourteenth day of the first moon after the vernal equinox, he saw Ra-min-ati. The streets of the royal city were thronged that day with visitors; all kinds of entertainment booths had been put up in the public park and arrangements made for music, dancing and games. This was a day for pleasure making in which the gay spirit of the Egyptians found expression through robust and spontaneous joy at the return of spring. The outer courts of the great temple were crowded; the people lined up for the grand procession. Ra-Hotep moved through this laughing crowd and passed the doors that led to the middle court, where the quiet of the inner temple enfolded him and an influence not of this world stole on his spirit, bringing peace.

He was in a ceremonial hall, its walls lined with gold. At the east end seven steps led to a golden altar on which stood a pair of seven-branched oil-lamps. In smaller alcoves, lamps were being lit by a slim, dark-haired young priestess who moved

silently on bare feet, clad in the traditional fine white linen of
her order. Ra-Hotep withdrew to the shadows near the entrance so that he could watch the graceful figure unseen. She
mounted the seven steps and lit the seven-branched lamps. As
she turned to descend he moved up the central aisle towards
her, noting how serene and happy she was. When she raised
her eyes and looked into his, a flash of recognition passed
between them; then once more all her attention and interest
were centred on her duties. In Ra-Hotep's eyes, she moved like
a figure in a dream as she passed him and disappeared through
a small door to the left of the altar. Thus, through a meeting
when no word was said, Ra-min-ati awakened something in
Ra-Hotep's heart. As surely as she had lit the lamps upon the
altar, she had kindled an inextinguishable light in the human
temple, the heart.

It was during this festival that the sacred vessel was taken
from the Holy of Holies to celebrate the resurrection of Osiris.
The immense doors of the inner courts were flung open and a
procession led by priests began its long perambulation through
the royal city and across the Nile in barges to the Valley of
Sleep. The priests carried emblems, including the ankh, key
of heaven and emblem of eternal life. Bearers followed with
the flags and symbols of the provinces of Upper and Lower
Egypt, then again temple musicians and trumpeters; preceded
by acolytes swinging censers, priests in ceremonial robes. Behind them came Pharaoh, carried in his litter by twenty-four
elders, surrounded and guarded by courtiers and soldiers.
He bore himself with high dignity and acknowledged the
obeisance and the cheers of his subjects by raising his right
hand in blessing.

After him came ladies of the court and young priestesses

from the temple, among whom Ra-min-ati's slim, dark-haired figure stood out for Ra-Hotep above all others.

The greater part of the people joined in the festivities of which this procession was the climax. Even the poorest brought some small offering to the souls of their dead, were it only a few flowers to show that love is stronger than death, the grave not a last resting-place. Twice a year the ceremony was enacted, at the vernal and autumnal equinoxes, which were regarded as symbolizing the soul's birth, first into this world of life and happiness, then into the greater happiness and freedom of life in the hereafter.

When the ceremonies were over the people were free to follow their own devices. Ra-Hotep, needing solitude that he might think about the young priestess, withdrew as soon as he could from the company in Pharaoh's court, and embarked. As his barge glided homeward the noise of tumult and revelry died down; the lapping water, the peace of a cloudless sky, seemed to beckon him into the enfolding silence of nature. Sweet night air bathed and cleansed his soul after the heat and excitement. Refreshed, he left the barge at the steps of the landing-stage and made his way through flower gardens towards his house of white stone. His servant, Ben Abou, watching for his arrival, led forward a fleet and graceful desert-horse, saddled and bridled: it was not unusual for Ra-Hotep to ride into the night on returning from his duties at Pharaoh's court. After an exchange of greetings, courteous enquiries about the day's events and a brief goodnight he was soon galloping along the desert's edge with only stars and a rising moon to guide him to a favourite cove on the riverbank. Here he liked to resort when some problem asked for solution; here more than anywhere he felt the presence of the invisible Ra.

Ever since he had watched the young priestess light the lamps that morning he had been asking himself, 'Who is she? Why did that flash of recognition pass between us?' He felt as certain that she knew him as he knew her—but where could they have met? He searched his memory, trying to recall some festival when it might have happened, but in vain.

He cantered along the riverbank for some time. The Nile was very wide here; small islands dotted the surface and made it look like a lake or inland sea under the night sky. Reaching his cove, he dismounted and stretched his tired body on the sands—lying on his back, hands clasped, gazing up at the moonlit and star-sprinkled sky, relaxed. He had never felt the mystery of life and the invisible so close. The love of the Mother of all things seemed to flow into him from the heart of nature, giving him silent and blessed companionship. Mingled with this was the memory of the girl in the temple, kindling the white-magical fire of love in his heart. 'How empty, how barren my life has been', he thought. 'I must have been waiting, waiting for someone I knew in the past, have always known perhaps, my soul's true companion whom I lost for a while.' He realized it was not only that a girl's beauty had unlocked his secret heart and reached into it; but spiritual consciousness had awakened, an inner awareness that brought with it ineffable, fragrant sweetness. 'It was like an initiation', he thought, 'an initiation into the sacred rites of the Temple of Ra'.

He spent hours in his retreat, dreaming, meditating, sleeping. Is-ra's face came often and vividly into his thoughts, and suddenly he made a decision. 'I'll go back to the city and seek audience with him. He will surely know who she is and tell me her name, tell me about her home and family. He may even arrange a meeting'. The idea so took possession of him that his second meeting with the priestess seemed an accomplished fact. He rose, remounted, turned the horse's head and cantered towards an outcrop of rock not far distant. During his solitary rides he had discovered a spacious and lofty cave hidden there, a retreat where he might camp for days at a time when he yearned for isolation and privacy. He had furnished it with bed, rugs, cushions and a collection of writings by Egypt's sages. When he made a lengthy stay, Ben Abou accompanied him and the servant always left a store of food and drink against his master's erratic retreats.

Tonight, having eaten and drunk, Ra-Hotep flung himself on the bed. Presently he fell asleep and dreamt a dream so vivid he could have sworn afterwards that he travelled back through past ages and relived another life in a tropical land such as he had never seen. Here people lived in high luxury. He saw women dressed in brilliant colours and wearing precious jewels, men in heavily-embroidered silk garments; sumptuous palaces with richest fabrics and carpets, stone and wood carvings inside and out. On the walls of galleries in a royal palace were paintings and bas-reliefs that depicted the splendours of those times; wall-paintings showed groups of dancers standing with arms entwined or holding bunches of flowers in their hands. He saw exotic gardens, artificial waterways, fountains and running streams having their source in purple mountains that towered over the city. The surrounding country was overwhelmingly rich with fruits, corn and vegetation. The seas supplied fish, the land flesh and fowl, enough for the biggest and most fastidious appetite.

Now Ra-Hotep saw himself attired in royal robes, seated on a golden throne on a dais; by his side, on a second throne, he saw the slight, royally dressed figure of his consort. Audi-

ence chamber and hall of justice were thronged with a brilliant
assembly. He received homage from a long line of people who
streamed past, turning constantly to his consort for comment
or advice on his greeting to some individual, on the meting-out
of justice or the granting of requests. Presently he awoke to
find himself back in the cave through whose entrance he saw
the first rays of dawn lighten the horizon. His waking could
only have lasted a few seconds, for next thing he was climbing
endlessly to the summit of a pine-clad mountain. Near the
top he came to an avenue of great trees unknown to him; and
this made his vision of some other land the more convincing,
a memory, it was clear, of yet another life in far off time and
space. Then as he walked in grassy avenues under the giant
trees the same slim figure came to him with eager, outstretched
hands, a white-clad figure whose dark hair was now encircled
with a golden band, jewel-studded, beneath which shone the
Egyptian priestess's bright, dark eyes. She turned with him to
retrace their steps to a stone temple at the end of a sunlit avenue
and as they approached it another man joined them. He too
was robed in white, girdled and embroidered with gold; and
he wore a high crown of white plumes banded and studded
with jewels. Again there was something familiar about him.
Ra-Hotep looked closer—surely he was not mistaken? The
eyes that greeted him were surely the kindly, humorous eyes
of the chief priest in the temple of Ra? It must be so. It was.
He called aloud, 'Is-ra! Is-ra!'.

His own cry awoke him and his dream quickly began to
fade, but not before his brain had received an impression of
that earlier life and dimly remembered it. Now he knew why
the girl priestess had enthralled him—was not she the consort
who sat beside him in his dream, the girl on the mountain?

*

The sun was high when Ra-Hotep rode into the city to seek audience with the chief priest. The morning ceremony of sun-worship was over and people were dispersing. As he entered the temple gardens he met Is-ra crossing the courtyard to one of the smaller council chambers. The priest greeted him. 'Your visit is no surprise to me', said Is-ra. 'I too dreamt last night.'

Ra-Hotep was amazed, delighted. Wonder on wonder, Is-ra must have read his mind and knew about the dream he thought was known only to himself. The high priest's eyes were twinkling as he listened to what Ra-Hotep said about his first glimpse of Ra-min-ati. 'She was lighting the altar lamps … there was something familiar about her figure and the way she moved, I couldn't withdraw my gaze. Then she turned to descend the steps and our eyes met and recognition dawned. In both of us, I'm sure of it.'

'Are you quite sure?' asked Is-ra.

'When can I meet her, speak to her?' the young man implored. 'My brain has been on fire since I saw her. I beg you to arrange a meeting. I shall have no peace until I can claim her as my bride.'

'Love is a delicate, rare flower that needs gentle handling. You recognized each other? How?'

'I remember her from a past life.'

'What proof have you?'

'I dreamed of lives together and I know I dreamed true. You too were in my dream and I know you can tell me who we were and what we all were to each other if you choose to do so.'

'It is not the will of the gods that I should open mysteries of the soul to you. Were I to do that I should rob you of one of the profoundest joys.'

'What joy?'

'The dawn of truth in the soul, self-discovery. Truth comes from your innermost consciousness, opening like a rose in sunlight. If I told you today all you want to know I should be guilty of mutilating the unfolding bud and there would be no flower. Have confidence in Ra's unfailing love.'

'But who is the priestess, Is-ra? At least give me her name that I may call to her in my dreams.'

'She is daughter to the priest Tahuti and Nofret, Pharaoh's sister. I shall have to seek their counsel and consent. Yes, I will try to arrange with Tahuti to meet you here within a month from now. Meanwhile you must return to your duties, my son.'

Ra-Hotep had to be content with this.

Chapter 13

Retrospect

LIFE had been ever more interesting to Ra-min-ati since Is-ra showed her the way into other worlds and how to recollect former lives. The present now filled only a small place in her mind. She thought about life, not in terms of immediate surroundings, but as a journey through many fascinating countries, meeting all kinds of people; a life so full that her happiness seemed complete, almost, but not entirely. She did not yet understand why this was so, but she felt there were realms still to be explored, wonders still to be experienced.

At the age of nineteen, when her seven-year apprenticeship was over, Ra-min-ati returned to her father's house, after full initiation as priestess. Later she devoted certain days to service in the temple, giving help and healing to those who sought it. Otherwise she was free to seek recreation in her home and its gardens, with her brothers, sisters and friends of her own age. She became fond of needlework and embroidery. She enjoyed helping her mother to prepare and preserve spices, fruits and vegetables and to make the sweetmeats and spiced sweet cakes for which the Egyptian housewife was renowned.

As part of her training Ra-min-ati had studied what we now call psychology, but it went deeper. Is-ra taught her how to project her soul in full consciousness out of the physical body into the world of spirit and move in it without restriction; how to read akashic records; how to diagnose sickness of the body which, in every case, he said, had its origin in the soul whether in this life or another. She was able to extend her vision beyond the scope of the uninitiated and see deep into the souls of those who visited the temple to worship or to consult her as priestess.

In time she became one of the oracles of the temple and men and women travelled long distances to seek her advice on material, psychological and spiritual problems. To acquire even the beginnings of such powers took long training in knowledge of the soul and understanding of the impulses and weaknesses of human nature; moreover, prolonged self-discipline was exacted before Ra-min-ati could receive from higher influences the wisdom to give true and helpful advice.

To initiate Ra-min-ati into the understanding of humanity's needs, Is-ra would send her away from the body on many and varied missions, so that she learnt how to enter the mind-and-soul consciousness of the man or woman she was to help. She learnt actually to suffer or rejoice by sharing their emotions and experiences.

For instance, when she was sent to awaken Zara in the spirit-world she saw the life Zara lived in her mud hut on the bank of the Nile, long, arduous days with many children, born in the space of a few years, clamouring to be clothed and fed, which involved much spinning of wool and weaving of flax for making garments. But Zara, though it meant unremitting toil, knew this was her karma and accepted it with submission, for which reason the gods sent a messenger to lighten the burden of her last years. While with Zara, Ra-min-ati felt every pang of the woman's sorrow, bore with her the weight of her slavery, the bitterness of unrealized hopes.

Thus, though Ra-min-ati lived a secluded life in the

sanctuary, she went out into the world to share other people's experiences. In fact their feelings were intensified for her as she became more highly receptive to psychic impressions. As the high priest explained, those who live or function mainly in the soul-world suffer more acutely than those who live in and for the body alone, a habit that dulls finer feelings. The coarser the body's vibration, the slower its receptiveness to intuitive truth.

Maidens dedicated to the temple learnt how to open their inner sight by meditation and by concentration on a globe or crystal. Vision awakened in this way was not limited to scenes of outward life; it sharpened gradually until it looked into the individual's emotional, mental and spiritual world. For example, Ra-min-ati could see what stage of unfoldment those who came to consult her had reached and divide them into two classes: those who had entered consciously into the stream of light; and those who, still unawakened, were confined to the material world in a state of spiritual darkness. Is-ra told her that these were not to be condemned or worse thought of than the others; both classes were to be regarded as brothers or sisters of her spirit, for all travelled the same road. If some were for the moment walking on the dark side of it, she must never forget that their blindness was temporary—she herself had walked the dark side in the past. In spirit and in essence they were as those who walked in the light.

'You see, Ra-min-ati', he said, 'one of the most important lessons to be learnt is how to transmute darkness or evil into light. Some people are called 'good', others 'evil'; but these words give a wrong idea. Good and evil are complementary. You will find it difficult to make people believe this; but darkness remains darkness until light disperses it, then it becomes light and truth. Darkness unredeemed by light is but one aspect of the reality and is called evil merely because light is absent. Those who are still ignorant of the law of karma cannot be called evil. Karma is the result and outworking of human action over a period short or long. The law that governs human life may be stated in the words, 'As a soul sows so it must reap'. Through experience, very painful experience sometimes, the soul learns not to inflict pain on others, knowing now that wilful cruelty, unkindness, selfishness, must in time rebound on the perpetrator, who will suffer the pain he or she inflicted.'

'Is there then no such thing as evil?', Ra-min-ati asked.

'What do you mean by 'evil'? Do you mean absence of knowledge?'

'Why, yes. I suppose that is what we call evil.'

'Do you blame a child because it lacked opportunity of learning a lesson?' asked Is-ra. 'You recognize that the child, as a child, is ignorant and you don't punish the child for it. Can you believe that anyone who once knew the light would or could still walk in darkness?'

'Is ignorance an excuse then for what is called evil?'

'No excuse, but the reason for it. Yet the soul is only ignorant once. Pain and suffering follows ignorance, bringing light and knowledge.'

'This should make us tolerant', Ra-min-ati remarked.

The priest smiled. 'Yes, and it brings vision. When we come to know the law that blends opposites, light and dark, good and evil, poverty and plenty, the sense of injustice and conflict disappears. We see only the outworking of perfect justice, bringing spirit or god-consciousness into manifestation.'

'How different life is, seen this way,' said Ra-min-ati. 'There was so much I thought I should never understand—now

I begin to see reason in everything.'

'Can you see what lies before you? You are to spend your days carrying light into the world, a task that the daily lighting of lamps in the sanctuary symbolizes. Remember the words, 'Let the light shine', that are chanted many times at the ceremony of the Light of Osiris. Here is the whole truth, Ra-min-ati. Here is the inner secret of white magic; to let the light which is knowledge, love, truth, shine in each human temple, each individual life. You haven't forgotten what happens on Midsummer Day in the Temple of Ra, when sunlight pierces the shadowed courts into the innermost precinct and shines on the sacred altar. This also symbolizes an eternal truth and mystery: the penetration of light into the darkest place and disappearance of darkness in light itself.'

'Is-ra....' Ra-min-ati hesitated. 'When I was lighting the lamps, a stranger stood watching me. At first I didn't know he was there, then it seemed as if I was compelled to look towards the west door. Our eyes met and I felt sure I knew him, although I couldn't remember having met him. I found out later that he is scribe to Pharaoh, because I saw him again, in the procession, walking immediately behind Pharaoh. I.... I was troubled. I would like to know more about him.'

'No doubt you will in good time. If you were so moved by a brief encounter there is every indication that you are age-old friends, destined to work together in this day of life.'

*

Two or three weeks later, when Ra-Hotep and Tahuti met, they recognized in each other the sign of true brotherhood in a secret Order, some knowledge of which has come down to this day. They knew it by sign and grip.

'I can see', said Is-ra, 'that no word from me is necessary, so I will leave you to fulfil Ra's law. We have all known Ra-min-ati through a number of incarnations; she has been daughter to me as well as pupil. She will meet you again in happiness, Ra-Hotep, and if Ra wills, bless the rest of your life on earth with her love.'

'May I be worthy of it!', exclaimed Ra-Hotep, marvelling at the high priest's words.

'If either of you needs my advice', added Is-ra, 'call me in thought. I shall hear and give such help as you can receive'. He lifted his hand. 'And now may Ra light your path and bless your life's work in his service.' He left them, giving each the sign and grip of that ancient Brotherhood.

Tahuti and Ra-Hotep boarded the state barge that would take them to Tahuti's house in silence; neither was in the habit of idle talk and on this occasion each was studying and 'sensing' the other's soul. But as they drew near their destination Tahuti broke silence and said, 'Nofret, my wife, will welcome you, Ra-Hotep.'

'I thank you both from my heart, Tahuti.'

In appearance and habit Tahuti resembled the Indians who sometimes came to Egypt in long, swift paddle-craft from the coast to trade gold for linens and gaily-coloured woollens. 'I have little to add to what Is-ra said', Tahuti answered. 'I have no doubt Ra-min-ati will welcome you also.'

'I fervently hope for it,' said Ra-Hotep.

The barge glided to the steps that led from the riverbank to the portico of the house where Nofret waited to receive them. The three greeted one another unaffectedly, accepting the situation. As they entered a spacious hall Ra-Hotep saw that the white marble floor, handsomely inlaid, was strewn with coloured rugs; he admired frieze and cornice of delicately-interlaced design embossed with gold, soft-coloured and embroidered curtains, divans and cushions, and heavy, carved chairs upholstered with tapestries. A few pieces of pottery holding sprays of flowering shrub or vine were set on low tables. The friendliness of the house greeted him, so that he 'felt' the personality of each member of this family and was refreshed by the peace and harmony of their home, as if he had stepped from the blazing heat of the desert into some cool and scented bower through which soft breezes played. 'This is a home indeed,' he thought. For many years he had wandered in loneliness, and now he had found a place of rest, where he might hear the gods whisper wisdom in the recesses of the heart. 'Here one might find the jewels of the spirit', he thought.

As soon as the two men had bathed away the dust of the city, Nofret served wine and cakes. Ra-Hotep noticed how slight and graceful she was, almost as young and lissom as her daughter. A woman who will never be called old, he told himself, for he saw that her mind was clear as crystal, active as her elegant little person, in spite of her cares and responsibilities. 'Now', she said, smiling at Ra-Hotep, 'if you are refreshed I expect you'd like to see Ra-min-ati. She has been in the garden nearly all morning. I think you'll find her on her favourite seat by the fountain and lotus pond. Tahuti, will you take Ra-Hotep to her?'.

Chapter 14

Reunion

IT SEEMED a long time to Ra-min-ati since that day in the temple when she first saw Ra-Hotep, and as the days passed she began to be impatient. 'How can I find out more about him?', she asked herself. 'He will probably leave the city and vanish from my life.' The idea filled her with a dismay that grew the more intense as she found how large a place he occupied in her mind; but she knew how necessary it was to control emotions that threatened her spirit, the true guide and counsellor whom Is-ra had been at such pains to teach her she must obey.

With such disquiets as these in her mind, she was sitting beside the pool in her father's garden, watching the birds. It was spring; the air she breathed pulsated with the same life-force as that which rose in the sap of tree, bush and flower. Soon the bushes and trees would blossom and the fertilisation of in-numerable blooms would follow; later the fruit, the completed life-effort of bush and tree, would appear. Then the sap would recede, down, down into the roots, to sleep in the arms of Isis. Year after year the same process; life would continue its rhythm of birth, death and rebirth through aeons of time.

What purpose lay behind this process of birth, life and death, change and decay, in all the kingdoms of nature? Where did it lead? Surely it was a manifestation and evolution of spirit buried in the darkness of matter and in human consciousness. She remembered Is-ra's words: 'In darkness is light; in the inanimate, life; in ignorance is unconscious knowledge'. If this were so, the spirit, not the body or human mind, could alone know life's aim.

Ra-min-ati heard voices. She glanced up to see her father with Ra-Hotep. For the second time she looked Ra-Hotep in the eyes and now she remembered him as an age-old comrade.

Tahuti said, 'I see you recognize each other'.

'Yes', answered Ra-Hotep. He took her hand and bowed over it, smiling. 'I have had the happiness of seeing Ra-min-ati before. She was lighting lamps in the temple but I couldn't speak to her.'

'Well, now is the opportunity,' said Tahuti. 'So if you'll excuse me I have some matters to attend to. I will join you later.'

Ra-Hotep turned to the girl. 'Since I first saw you', he said, 'you have been ceaselessly in my thoughts'.

'And you in mine', she returned.

'I can't tell you why it is so,' said Ra-Hotep, still in a daze, when at last they found speech, 'but I know for certain, I have known for a long time that we are age-old friends'.

'I know this too, but where we were together is still a mystery', she said.

They wandered along a flower-walk into Ra-min-ati's garden where she came when she desired meditation, and seated themselves by a fountain whose waters tinkled into a pool and lotuses rested their white and gold heads on the surface. They watched the drops from the fountain fall glistening in sunlight. Invited by their silence and stillness, fairies, water-sprites and elves swung from flower to flower and played hide-and-seek among grasses that fringed the pool. 'Can you see them?', she asked, noticing his spellbound face.

'I'm seeing them for the first time since I was a boy', Ra-Hotep replied; then, after a pause, 'My sisters and I used to be quite familiar with them when we were children, but I had almost forgotten such creatures existed. And you, can you always see into the land of sunlight?'

'Yes. I suppose I've grown so used to looking into a world within this that the two have become one. Now I can't imagine what it would be like if I could see only the denser aspect of things. I should feel like someone blind who can sense beauty and smell the scent of flowers but can't see them.'

Ra-Hotep knew that there were people who had inner sight such as this and that temple-training was designed, among other things, to promote its development; but not for a long time had he talked with anyone whose third eye was open to see as Ra-min-ati saw. Once again they fell silent, she watching the capers of the little people, fascinated, he studying with covert glances every line of her face. Not only was she graceful and beautiful, but an embodiment of peace and harmony such that her companionship was precious and utterly satisfying. Only a short time since Ra-Hotep first touched Ra-min-ati's hand and he had no doubt at all that here beside him sat the comrade of his spirit, for whom he had longed many lonely years, knowing she awaited him somewhere.

Perhaps in answer to an unspoken question Ra-min-ati broke silence. 'We can't see the place where we last met, just now. But Is-ra said, "Time will uncover the past". When the gods permit, the secret will be shown us. How did you find out who I am and where I live?'.

'I asked Is-ra. He is my father's friend.'

'You came back to the temple then?'

'Yes. Is-ra befriended me before I left home on foreign

service. I knew I could open my heart to him and he would perhaps help me to find you. I met him crossing the temple court. There seemed no need to explain myself—he knew what I wanted. Today he presented me to your father. We became friends at once and ... here I am!'. He paused. 'But it isn't quite all the story. I had two vivid dreams. Both seemed so real I prefer to call them experiences.' And he went on to tell her all he could remember of his glimpses into a life lived in a land where he recognized her as his consort.

Ra-min-ati understood perhaps better than he the meaning of his vision. Interrupting, she told him his second dream when they met in a temple among the pines on a mountain and Is-ra was with them. She sat for a while with closed eyes and suddenly opened them. 'Yes', she said with conviction, we were brother and sister in that life. Is-ra was our father'. Ra-Hotep could not doubt words or vision. And what more could he ask than to sit with her in this quiet place, alive with the girl he loved?

As they talked he saw more and more clearly that he had remembered in dream a life lived long ago. Until now he had been unsettled, lost, always looking for something vital that was missing. Even the time he spent in the desert and beside the Nile had failed to supply it. But now happiness was opening his heart, the past came flooding back so that, like Ra-min-ati, he knew the quality of their true relationship. Life in the fullness of its possibilities had only now begun. Until today he had spent his days doing work for work's sake, living without deeper incentive or happiness. Now everything was changed. 'When I first saw you in the temple I knew you were part of me', he said, his eyes resting on the dark head.

'I knew it too. But I couldn't remember then where we

met. Now I remember more clearly, but still not perfectly. I see us among trees and high mountains and there's a white stone temple on the mountain, and priests in white and gold robes. And there was someone else whom we loved.'

'I too have that impression', Ra-Hotep agreed. 'If he saw fit I think Is-ra could help clear our sight.'

After another and longer silence when language seemed inadequate for their thoughts and their thoughts faded into contentment, clasping his hand Ra-min-ati said, 'Since we met I have known more and more certainly a life that isn't limited by time or space. You have brought the world of spirit nearer than ever it was before. I feel as though together, we generate a power that links us with universal and eternal life. You remember? On the mountain where that white temple stood the priests spoke of the Great White Light. They said it was magic, Ra's love made manifest. They told us many things about the magical power of love. They said the deeper and truer the love between two people the more imperative it became that the magic circle should expand and draw others in.'

She paused and continued as if she were thinking aloud. 'Who can tell, how deep an impression, love that arises from the union of two souls can make? May not its influence persist far beyond one life and affect innumerable lives in generations unborn? Its power lives eternally, ever increasing its influence, ever radiating truth, beauty, happiness. But what comes of selfishness, harshness, cruelty, ugliness, hate, can't live long and is sooner or later consumed in its own fires'.

Ra-Hotep listened and loved her with all his being. 'We are generating and feeling the power at this moment', he said. 'If it is as strong as this at our first meeting we must be going to do some work together. I wonder what lies before us?'

Thus they talked, sitting hand in hand while the fountain played in the garden. They talked so long that they forgot time until a servant came out to call them.

Nofret and Tahuti were happy too, for they knew that Ra-min-ati had met one whom she loved and whose love would enrich her life. Tahuti had told Nofret how Is-ra had sent for him and said, 'Long ago Ra-Hotep was my son. He knows in himself what his mission is, but he is still unawakened. The meeting with Ra-min-ati will soon stir his memory and the curtain that now shuts out the past will be lifted. They were both my children, brother and sister. Now they have met again their life's work will begin in earnest … until now they have been on probation.'

It is hardly surprising then that Nofret welcomed her guest with deepest sincerity and invited him to remain with them some days. He spent as much time as he could with Ra-min-ati, sailing on the river, visiting cities and temples on its banks, exploring the countryside.

The room where the family dined adjoined the reception hall and was equally spacious. The walls were similarly decorated with paintings of gatherings, feasts and scenes with dancers and musicians. The religious aspects of life were shown; for while the Egyptians believed in extracting the maximum of enjoyment from the things of this world they never forget that life is transitory. Very often an effigy of Osiris was brought out at a party to remind people of the life after death.

The family dined at a round table supported by a central pedestal in the form of a twining snake. They used embroidered napkins, carved ivory spoons for soup, a knife to cut meat that they conveyed to the mouth with their fingers. Dinner on this occasion consisted of soup, fish, fowl, followed by grapes, figs, dates fresh and dried, nuts, raisins and pomegranates, which servants brought in great baskets. They drank wine or beer from alabaster cups or beakers. Ra-Hotep felt he had reached new heights of enjoyment in surroundings and company.

Chapter 15

Ra-Hotep is Called to the Temple

IS-RA knew the time had come for Ra-Hotep to be established in the position it had been decreed he should hold, for these things are planned long before they happen on earth. He decided therefore to ask Pharaoh, his close friend, to give the young man an appointment carrying authority to govern the people on lines similar to those with which he was intuitively familiar from his life among the Mayas. Clear memory of it would come to him with the passing of time.

A sinister influence had been creeping into the court and government circles. It originated perhaps through the marriage of certain officials with women of a neighbouring country, and gave rise to much intrigue, with growing love of wealth and personal power. Thus some of the higher officials sought to dominate the weaker section of the community. This had a demoralising effect in royal circles and among civil servants and governors in the Nomes. Is-ra pointed out to Pharaoh the urgent need for vigilance and wise handling. As his own work was primarily to do with the religious education of temple pupils and the conduct of royal ceremonies, he was unable to take on additional duties; but he received intimation from the Master that Ra-Hotep would be suitable for appointment as Overseer and Adviser to the Council of Provincial Governors.

Pharaoh listened attentively while Is-ra made this proposal and told of Ra-Hotep's training in a past incarnation and his military record in this present life. Is-ra considered no one in the court better qualified for such a post. Pharaoh dismissed him with a promise that he would meditate on it.

Thus, while he was still at Ra-min-ati's home, Ra-Hotep received from Is-ra a summons to the temple in the royal city. 'I suppose I must obey', he said. 'I can't imagine why I'm sent for, but there it is. I must answer it.'

Ra-min-ati felt certain its purpose was to open up a plan for their life and work, but she said nothing.

The night before Ra-Hotep's departure, he dreamt he was once again in another strange yet vaguely familiar land, familiar because the buildings, temples and monoliths resembled Egypt's, and he met Ra-min-ati, Is-ra, Nofret and Tahuti there. He stood in the centre of a group of people in white robes wearing headdresses of plumes, receiving instruction in the laws of the Brotherhood and how to apply them in matters of government. 'For this is what lies immediately before you', Is-ra was saying. 'You are shortly to be appointed to a position which will bring you into close relationship with Pharaoh. You will be in his confidence and you will be able to restore to the land of Khem some of the ancient laws of brotherhood and just rule.'

Awakening with a vivid impression of the dream, Ra-Hotep wondered what it portended. Loath to part from Ra-min-ati, not knowing when they would meet again, he comforted himself with the thought that if the summons to the city had some bearing on the future it might bring marriage nearer.

On arrival at the temple he was admitted to the presence of the chief priest, who stretched out his hands in welcome. Is-ra saw by the light in Ra-Hotep's face that love, bringing expansion of consciousness, had lifted Ra-Hotep to the heights of happiness. This gave him satisfaction, for it would sharpen the young man's perceptions and increase his capacity to govern. 'I have received a summons to attend Pharaoh and to bring you with me', Is-ra said. 'I am aware of what has taken place since our last meeting and your happiness increases my own.'

Ra-Hotep remembered again his dream of the previous night and Ra-min-ati's description of their meeting in the Temple of the Pines, high up on the mountain in the Land of the West. He remembered that Is-ra had been there while he was instructed in the lore of the White Brotherhood. Was he now to receive some appointment commensurate with his dreams? Were his most ardent hopes to be realized? If so, would Ra-min-ati and he soon marry, live in their own home, work together? 'May I know what is in your mind concerning this summons?', he asked.

'Dissatisfaction is growing among the people, who resent unjust handling of their concerns in the law-courts, and the ever-growing taxation that provincial governors exact of them. News of this has reached Pharaoh, and he is determined to stop discord and discontent from spreading. He is thinking of appointing an adviser, who would also be overseer of the provincial councils. It is possible that you will receive the appointment.'

Ra-Hotep's eyes shone. 'This is work after my own heart!', he cried. 'Ra-min-ati has stirred up memories of our past together and I'm beginning to see that the work of the White Brotherhood may be done in this land. I see the guiding hand of those who are great and wise. It is a wonderful opportunity and with the guidance and help of the Brothers of the Light we shall succeed.'

'It won't be a path strewn with flowers', Is-ra remarked, knowing well what lay ahead. 'You must be prepared for obstruction in certain quarters as well as active and bitter opposition from many whom you number among your friends and who will become your enemies. Disappointment, frustration, will attend you. For a time, a long time perhaps, you will be unpopular with most and hated by some.'

'I'm ready to face all that,' declared Ra-Hotep.

'Very well, I have warned you and I include Ra-min-ati in the warning. You will both meet opposition, but you will have compensations—your mutual love, your home life in growing happiness. Ra tests and blesses those who love and serve him. If you keep steadfastly to the appointed path, caring for neither praise nor blame, you will reap the fruits of your labours. But I repeat: there will be hard and bitter struggles and some defeats. It is useless to enter the public service with selfish motives: if you do, you will be doomed to lamentable failure. Courage and selflessness are the friends you will need in your office if you are to achieve what you hope for.'

'I am profoundly grateful for what you have said. I realize what difficulties will beset me. But I still wish to accept this opportunity if it is to be offered me.'

Is-ra looked at the straight figure with affection. Rising, he put a hand on the young man's shoulder and said, 'I shall advise Pharaoh to appoint you'.

*

Pharaoh received his counsellors in a lofty hall whose walls and ceiling were decorated with figures of ships, animals, flowers, fruits and heavenly beings in rich, soft colours. Red columns, carved at the foot to resemble the roots of trees, the column itself, as it were a trunk with branches and leaves of gold spreading across the ceiling, supported the roof. Entering, one seemed to be in a forest of golden trees whose trunks were covered in red bark. The hall was illuminated from the roof and from cleverly devised openings in the walls—the light shining like sunlight where needed, leaving the rest in a subdued glow. This made an atmosphere conducive to the clear vision needed in formulating laws for the wellbeing of the people.

At the eastern end, on a handsomely carved throne raised on three golden steps, sat Pharaoh. Advancing in years, he bore on his face the marks of a strong, resolute character. Rich in human experience, he was known as a man of strict self-discipline who could be stern, even severe, with his subordinates when occasion called for it. He had keen perceptions and a subtle appreciation of human nature in its aspirations as well as its weaknesses. As Priest-Pharaoh to be, he had passed through the temple training in his earlier years and was well versed in the Ancient Wisdom.

Ra-Hotep followed Is-ra into the golden hall. Both bowed low before the royal figure who stretched out a hand to each in turn, whereon each pressed his lips on it and withdrew a few paces. Although Ra-Hotep was already known to Pharaoh, he felt himself under scrutiny so thorough that his whole life was laid bare; and subterfuge, if he ever resorted to it, would be useless. Pharaoh himself recognized in the man before him one who was destined to rule and lead. He liked the dignified bearing, the resolute, lighted face. He perceived a quality that would justify the placing of responsibility on it. He knew how rare it was to find a man who possessed the combination of qualities the work he had in mind would require, and what he read in Ra-Hotep's soul pleased him. 'My son', he said, 'unhappiness, discontent, hardship and suffering in some cases, due to unjust taxation and petty tyranny on the part of those having authority in provincial government, are corroding the lives of my people. I will not allow this to continue. The source of this evil must be traced and eliminated. The people must be firmly established in brotherhood throughout the land. Evil can spread like a poisonous weed that takes root in one night and smothers fair growth. Unless it is uprooted and burnt, it will bring about total destruction. The task of eliminating this weed is one for which I see you are well fitted. You will be given absolute authority. It will be for you to investigate, uproot and find a way of protecting the people in the future. You will take up your appointment on the day of the new moon.'

Ra-Hotep bowed and kissed Pharaoh's hand. Is-ra stepped forward, a hand resting on Ra-Hotep's shoulder. 'There is another matter that requires sanction, Your Holiness', he said.

'Speak on.'

'I bring word from your royal sister, Nofret. It concerns her daughter, Ra-min-ati, who has been my pupil these seven years. Nofret asks your consent to the marriage of Ra-min-ati with Ra-Hotep. Now that you have appointed him to this post, may he make your sister's daughter his bride?'

'What do the records of these two young lives tell us?' Pharaoh asked.

'That they were brother and sister in the Land of the West and in that life they were my son and daughter. When I left my body for the land of our forefathers they continued to guide and govern our people according to the laws of the Brotherhood of the Plumed Serpent.'

At this Pharaoh's face lighted with an ineffable sweetness. He took Ra-Hotep's hands in his and held them, on which the young man fell on his knees and Pharaoh, High Priest, blessed him with the love of Ra.

On leaving the palace Is-ra bade Ra-Hotep return to his own home, there to await the royal warrant appointing him to his duties in Upper Egypt. 'I will tell Ra-min-ati and her parents the good news', he said. 'In the meantime, there is much for you to meditate.'

Ra-Hotep was glad of the opportunity to think over the implications of these swift-moving events. Ra-min-ati had shown him how to rise into planes of higher consciousness and revive memories of past lives, so that the memory of his life as a Maya chief came back in full, and the plan of government the priests of the White Magic had taught him grew even clearer in his mind than when he was living there. He saw that the first essential in welfare and happiness was that government should stand on spiritual law. Unless this was understood and applied from the ruler down to every detail in the community's life there could only be chaos and unhappiness. To eliminate selfishness, he must first inculcate an ideal of brotherhood, draw people together in small groups, and show them how to tune themselves individually with the plane of spirit. Laws intended to safeguard their rights must be drawn up in conformity with the laws of brotherhood; otherwise officials would be tempted by love of power and ideals would vanish, deterioration would follow. What he learnt in his daily meditation with Ra-min-ati and from the priests of the White Light must prove of infinite value now. His companionship with Ra-min-ati had been long enough to give him a fairly comprehensive understanding of the basis of true government, so that he had been ready for his meeting with Pharaoh and knew enough to inspire his confidence.

He knew well now that without Ra-min-ati he could not recover the qualities past experience had developed in him, that were necessary for his coming task. She had given him more than he had acquired during the whole of his life. The child of true companionship between a man and a woman is not always a child of flesh and blood; it may be spiritual, creative. The union of two souls, the joining of spirit with spirit, can be quite as important as human marriage: but it is not given to everyone to win the blessings of love on all the planes of being.

Chapter 16

Fulfilment

SOME days later, sitting in the portico that faced the river, Ra-Hotep was immersed in work when Ben Abou appeared and handed him a papyrus. He broke the seal of the temple and read eagerly.

Is-ra wrote to say that Pharaoh consented to Ra-Hotep's marriage with Ra-min-ati. The letter went on, 'Within two months of the ceremony and on your appointment as Counsellor, you are to bring her to the palace and receive the royal warrant. She will be called on to undertake special duties at court, so arrangements for your marriage should be made at once'. Is-ra added, 'I am consulting Tahuti and Nofret about date and time. You may now visit Ra-min-ati in her father's house and arrange the details.'

Ben Abou, watching, saw that the papyrus contained something important. 'I am to be married,' Ra-Hotep explained. Ben Abou prostrated himself, then bowed many times, to show his pleasure. 'We have much to do in a short time, Ben Abou', Ra-Hotep said. 'Everything must be perfect.' And he lost no time making the journey to Tahuti's house, where a family conference was held. 'In less than a month', he suggested, 'the ceremonies of the summer solstice will be held. Wouldn't it be fitting that our wedding should take place on Midsummer Day? The moon will be full'.

This was agreed. Ra-min-ati's many friends helped in the

preparation of wedding-clothes and spent many hours cutting and sewing. Sometimes the girls listened to music, or danced and sang, for the time of preparation was held to be one of the happiest in a bride's experience. The pure white silk from which the bridal dress was made came from India as a present to Nofret, Pharaoh's sister. Ra-min-ati's wedding would rank as the wedding of a member of the royal house and take place in the temple of Ra. Pharaoh himself would be present.

According to custom, a party was held on the eve of the ceremony. The guests, seated at numerous small tables, were served with roast duck, goose, ox, veal, and all kinds of vegetables. Then came fruit-bearers who placed baskets filled with pineapples, pomegranates, grapes, figs, dates and passion fruit; then wine-bearers appeared with choice vintages. The bridal pair were seated with their relations at a long table at the upper end of the hall. During the feast musicians played on flutes and stringed instruments. Later the temple dancers, showing graceful figures through their diaphanous garments, entertained the guests, who themselves joined in the dancing-out of sheer gaiety.

They had brought wedding-presents, jewellery, embroidery, fine linen and works of art, as an expression of thankfulness to Ra for the beneficence of the gods towards the couple. The gifts were displayed in a spacious alcove, while in another Ra-Hotep and Ra-min-ati received congratulations and good wishes when their friends left.

The day following, Ra-min-ati dressed in her wedding-gown, embroidered around the neck and on the train with lotuses. She wore a crown of amethysts, sapphires, chrysolites and rubies in the form of the ankh. A gossamer veil fell over head and shoulders, reaching to the hem of her gown; this too was embroidered in silks of colours that matched the gems in her headdress, patterned with birds, butterflies and flowers, sylphs, water-sprites, gnomes and salamanders.

Accompanied by her parents, her eyes alight, she was carried in a litter to the royal barge; thronging, jubilant crowds attended their progress. First in the procession of barges came Ra-min-ati with her retinue, then Nofret with her husband and younger children, then the senior priests with younger priests and priestesses who had been sent to escort the bride. The leading barge was painted in colours representing the summer solstice, with all the hues and life-giving properties of the sun and the divine mother. The barges following had awnings of canvas dyed orange, flame and yellow mixed with bright green. Smaller craft swarmed in their wake.

At the temple, a fanfare of trumpets heralded Pharaoh's arrival. He was received by Is-ra and other priests, who conducted him to a golden chair of state. Ra-min-ati too was received with trumpets and strains of music from an orchestra of harps, other stringed instruments and flutes. Having made obeisance to Pharaoh, she paced slowly between the standing courtiers to steps that led up to the high altar, shining with gold and ablaze with lamps, over which hung the winged, golden disc of the Sun. The air was heavy with a sweet smell of incense and temple singers joined with the orchestra in a paean. It faded as Ra-min-ati came to Ra-Hotep's side. The chief priest blessed them and joined their hands.

Now two golden rings were handed to Is-ra on a cushion. He raised them before the altar, and prayed to Ra to bless these symbols of marriage in body, soul and spirit between this man and this woman and consecrate it, after which they received the rings and made vows. Is-ra, raising both arms, called on the host of witnesses visible and invisible to enfold the couple in the light of the Eternal: and many thought they saw the divine light envelop them at this moment.

The ceremony over, they made obeisance to Pharaoh, seated there in his golden chair, surrounded by nobles and attendants. As Priest of the Sun, he laid his hands on their heads as they knelt, and joined their hands in token of love and companionship. Pharaoh then bowed to the Supreme and held out a hand first to the one, then to the other; each raised it to the forehead. Then at a sign, they rose and retired, still facing him, nor did they turn to the great doors of the temple until he too rose. They went hand-in-hand through the congregation, all of them bowed in prayer, and out into sunshine.

Soldiers kept back the cheering crowds that were awaiting this moment. Again and again the trumpets blared out, while the bridal chariot was pelted with white flowers as it went through crowded streets amid music and laughter. A procession followed, some people in chariots, some riding, others walking, dancing and singing. The brothers and sisters of the couple, their friends, temple dancers and musicians, all streamed to the landing-stage where a gaily decked barge awaited. Here the two said goodbye to family and friends.

A measure of sadness tinged Ra-min-ati's joy, for all her past life as a child, novice and priestess seemed to recede, while the quay from which relatives still waved melted into distance. She turned with a sigh and looked south where, on the east bank of the Nile, she could see the white house that was to be her new home. As they approached, the sinking sun burnished walls and gardens, so that it seemed to stand in the golden heart of light. Ra-Hotep was at her side while the barge slowed to the steps and as they entered the house his arm encircled her and drew her close.

*

During four weeks whose memory was a bright jewel in the happiness that crowned Ra-min-ati's life, golden sunsets across the Nile glowed with more than natural beauty. They displayed such power and glory within the sun that when she stood in silence with Ra-Hotep she was at one with Ra, supreme Source of life.

The outer world had no existence just now for these two. But they were soon to be reminded that human affairs do not wait; for one morning, when they were enjoying the flowers and flowering trees, admiring a vista of pools and little blue lakes in the soft green of trees and lawns, Ben Abou came to announce a messenger from the chief priest. They went back to the house, both guessing the purport of the message, both knowing their days of undivided happiness and refreshment were drawing to a close, both understanding and accepting it that a life of arduous work and continual responsibility lay before them.

They were summoned to the royal city. Ra-min-ati smiled. Both were so imbued with the spirit of service that they readily answered the call, knowing that in the end they would find deeper happiness in service than in their own pleasures. The following day they went by barge to meet the chief priest.

Is-ra was waiting for them. When greetings and enquiries were over, he told them they were to receive the seal of office from Pharaoh on the third day of the new moon. He explained that it was planned to make a state occasion of the appointment, and they would be expected to prepare themselves for it by fasting and meditation. On the third day of the new moon they drove to the palace by a broad road that, since word of what was in progress had reached the people, was lined with thousands of men, women and children. They entered the palace by a portico over which the head of a lion was carved, and passed through the Court of Justice into the Hall of Initiation, whose massive doors closed behind them. At the eastern end they mounted seven steps the breadth of the hall to a dais where Pharaoh, surrounded by counsellors and priests, sat enthroned on a carved stone seat whose arms were draped with sun-coloured silks.

The ceremony was known as the Initiation of the Second Degree, its purpose to attune the candidates and make them receptive to the guidance of those in the invisible world who were to help them. A candidate was required to show proficiency in the intricacies of Egyptian law and familiarity with the principles underlying popular education, culture, art, agriculture; also domestic and religious life. Ra-Hotep was of course versed in such matters as the discipline and training of soldiers. He was qualified to sit in the Elders' council-chamber, having served a period as scribe at court, when he studied law. Ra-min-ati had qualified herself by seven years of temple discipline, by practice in reading the soul and in the art of communication in full consciousness with the inner worlds and after-death life. Thus they were both fitted for the responsibilities that were to devolve on them.

In silence, the officiants grouped themselves round the throne, and Pharaoh rose to his feet. Raising both arms he called on Ra, life-giver, to receive into his keeping the souls of these two mortals now to be dedicated as servants to the Egyptian people. Both knelt before Pharaoh in token of humility and surrender to the supreme King. In the ensuing silence the presence of invisible beings could be felt, from the spirits of the elements to those highest in the angelic hierarchy, come to assist their human brethren. Though the ceremony was simple and few words were spoken, it brought about an expansion of consciousness in the two candidates. This expansion gave them deeper insight into human need, as they opened their souls to the light and power that poured on them from the Sun-Ra.

At length, Pharaoh came down from the dais, took them by their hands and bade them rise. He held two jewels, each set in a scarab and suspended on a fine gold chain, on the back of the scarab a hieroglyph which meant, 'In love I serve'. Pharaoh looked long at the jewels, and with emotion, before he invested first Ra-min-ati, then Ra-Hotep, in recognition of the fact that they had been dedicated by Pharaoh himself as Ra's agent. Then, at a signal, the tylers opened the temple doors and Pharaoh led the way to the outer court where he presented the initiates to the people.

Amid renewed cheers, the waving of orange blossoms and palm leaves, and to strains of music, Ra-Hotep and Ra-min-ati entered a chariot which drove them by an avenue that was flanked either side with stone images of the gods and goddesses and other massive carvings, to their new house in the royal city. This was to be their official residence except for when they found time to rest in their riverside home, free from all pomp and ceremony.

*

During the next ten years Ra-Hotep, helped by his wife, instituted reforms that established him in the people's hearts as a wise and loved protector. He and Ra-min-ati had also been allowed to revive memories of the past still further and to pursue their work on the inner planes with the Brotherhood of the White Magic. By this means, Ra-Hotep came to understand the full purpose of his mission, which was none other than to form a brotherhood similar to the one established on earth long since by the sages of the west.

In the early days of his office, guided by the invisible Brotherhood, he gathered together men and women qualified to form the new Lodge. Some were called, others offered themselves. On initiation, all were made to understand what was required of them, to realize that the Brotherhood aimed at giving both personal and impersonal service to the community. Thus, the first qualification for membership was purity of motive with the sincere desire to transcend egoism—which is, as they were taught, the most formidable barrier to spiritual attainment. The light of Ra can only be sent out when the lower self, selfishness in the very heart, is overcome. Each initiated brother or sister was taught also that there is in the soul a certain quality which can be used, when combined with a like quality in other brethren, to radiate into the world a light which stimulates the best in human kind. The importance of the individual effort of each brother or sister, and their personal responsibility to the community, was stressed. Brotherhood was open to men and women alike; anyone might apply. The candidate must then prove to be a true aspirant to the supreme Light by self discipline and service to the poor and the sick.

A small Lodge of initiates of the white magic was thus formed. The spiritual power of the group took shape like a six-pointed star whose light could be projected to any human being, as they willed. In meditation and thought-projection the brothers and sisters created a picture of the six-pointed star and radiated its light into the darkest places of Egypt, to comfort the sorrowful, to light the way, to inspire loving, just and creative thoughts. This was but a beginning, the foundation of a powerful organisation whose influence was to bring, among other things, better and happier living and working conditions to the people. It was followed by the formation of similar groups throughout the two lands, and as the result of persistent steady work the lot of the poor gradually improved and the lives of the rich were changed by a knowledge that taught understanding, kindness and tolerance. In time, the effects of the influence began to be seen in the entire social, political, cultural and religious life of the people. It can be said that the Egyptian people attained at that time a degree of happiness such as had not been known since the days when the wise ones came from the motherland of the West.

Chapter 17

Music and Healing

TOWARDS the end of the second year of Ra-min-ati's marriage, a daughter was born, to whom the name Ati was given. The child grew to be an embodiment of the love and happiness that had blessed her parents. Dark eyes, rosy cheeks and dark brown hair proclaimed Ati a true daughter of the Sun, loving life, loving her companions, loving nature whether the flowers, birds and animals or the fairies. Even when a baby she would lie in the sun, thrusting out her limbs in sheer joy of movement, gurgling and talking to the fairies, air-sprites and gnomes that gathered round her. She would try to catch the fairies that fluttered like butterflies beyond her reach, and she would chuckle at the sylphs when they flew right into her face, only to dart off again with the speed of thought. At an early age she showed aptitude in modelling clay miniatures of animals, birds and flowers. She liked also to play with coloured bricks, building pyramids and columns or houses with gardens into which she put little figures to represent their inhabitants, and amused herself with her families for hours, never seeming to feel lonely.

When she was three years old, a brother was born and he was given the name Nuki. Very early he showed a decided taste for music, so Ra-Hotep gave him a small lute and taught him to use it. He soon began to play simple tunes, and when he was seven or eight he and Ati would go off into the marshes that fringed the Nile, where he would play his lute or embark on some adventure with his sister—who filled the most ordinary game with people of high rank and quality. The two children would paddle about for hours on the shallow marshes in a punt, living in a make-believe and fairy-like kingdom. They were always accompanied by Ben Abou, who was sometimes allowed to share their adventures.

In his early years Nuki showed skill with wind as well as stringed instruments. He was not merely content to produce harmonious sounds, but wanted to understand how they could be drawn out of silence, as if he had inkling of some magical secret to which music was the key. His father once found him banging pieces of metal with a stick in such a manner as to produce certain notes. Once he was discovered trying to make himself a stringed instrument by tying catgut to a piece of wood. It soon became clear that no vocation other than music would satisfy him.

One day when Ra-min-ati and her children were in the garden, Nuki was engaged in cutting and shaping a reed to make a flute, Ati absorbed in some embroidery. When the flute was ready, Nuki blew a few notes and shouted with excitement at the result of his first attempt to create music on an instrument of his own fashioning. Ati dropped her work and ran to him with arms outstretched, crying, 'Oh, let me try too'. Somewhat reluctantly, Nuki handed his treasure to his sister who found with a few moments' practice that she could pipe an Egyptian folk-tune. 'Make me another flute', she insisted, 'and we'll play together'. Delighted, he cut a flute that proved even better than the first and the two of them spent hours learning the new art, so that in time they could pipe to the accompaniment of birdsong and so improved with experience that one day some scores of birds watched them from the trees. 'Let's see if we can draw them closer', Nuki proposed. They played on, fascinated, evidently giving the birds pleasure, for some fluttered down to rest on their heads, shoulders or arms, or gathered round in a circle.

Another day when they were in the garden and Ati had finished practising, she went to gather up her embroidery and felt a severe sting. She cried out. Ra-min-ati ran to her, examined the embroidery and found a small scorpion in its folds. By now, as the girl's arm was swelling alarmingly, her mother began to suck out the poison. Having extracted the worst of it, she sent an attendant in haste for the priest-healer and a musician. Meanwhile Nuki and she carried Ati into the house and laid her on a couch in their healing sanctuary, which they called the blue room.

The healer concentrated his gift on the poisoned arm for some hours, until the inflammation subsided and the limb was healed. During this long concentration the musician and Nuki played the flute and the lyre to aid him: it was Nuki's first experience of the power music can lend to the healing art.

The sunlit years of childhood slipped away, and when the time came for Ati and Nuki to undergo temple training, Ra-min-ati took them to Is-ra, so that he could investigate the record of their past lives and see what the future would bring. By this means he would make certain they would receive the education that best suited them and assure their mental and spiritual growth.

It was decided that Ati was to follow the same course of training as Ra-min-ati had received, for the girl possessed qualities that would make her apt for service in the Temple of Ra. She was therefore put in the care of a priest-astrologer, As-ra.

Nuki was advised to study music, Is-ra having concluded that the boy was in affinity with the Venusian ray, which governs music and art. He became a student at the Hall of Music, under an old priest named Horem-Heb. Although this man was no easy character, being somewhat of a recluse, inclined to be gruff and thus frequently misunderstood by his pupils, a close friendship arose between these two. Horem-Heb was so absorbed in music, which he made into a kind of spiritual science, that he often seemed wholly detached from human interests and friendly intercourse. It rather surprised his colleagues therefore when he began to show a particular interest in Nuki. Entirely unselfconscious, the boy recognized in the priest, a teacher who could and would impart knowledge, and he became greatly attached to the old man. The two spent hours experimenting with the reeds that grew plentifully along the creeks, and Nuki learnt how to cut them so as to make flutes of various special types. In this and other ways the development of his precious gift was encouraged.

'Music is white magic which the gods use to bless and heal men and women', said Horem-Heb. 'You have found you can attract birds with it. This happens with the nature-spirits as well; when the little people hear strains of music apt to their nature and understanding, they answer at once. Then they can be directed by one of their angelic leaders, who has also been drawn by the music and works under the priest-healer's control. Yes, music is magic and the gods use it. There is power in it to heal, to raise human aspirations. It can lighten the wayfarer's burden and uplift the soul, so that it finds peace and blessedness in the arms of the Mother Isis. It rests with each person to develop and perfect this gift.'

Nuki found that music played a large part both in temple

healing and in the unfoldment of an aspirant's spiritual powers. The Egyptian teachers had learnt that rays of healing from the sun could be gathered by the healer and concentrated on the patient; and that the effectiveness of this method could be enhanced by vibrations of music. They knew that music produces vibrations in the fine ethers as one colour or another which supplies some element lacking in the patient's etheric body—bringing about a more harmonious condition, which is communicated in due course to the flesh-and-blood body and restores it.

Chapter 18

The Law of Love

TWELVE years had passed since Ra-Hotep formed the first Lodges of the White Brotherhood. After some initial sifting, an inevitable part of the process of trial and error, the people themselves joined heartily in every effort to improve their conditions; thus, the work of the Brotherhood so long concentrated on Ra-Hotep's people ultimately brought them happiness and plenty. Men and women began to realize that wise rulership and their own welfare depended not only on Pharaoh and the provincial governors but on some factor that lay hidden in themselves as well.

Thus they came to accept the necessity of a spiritual rather than a material conception of wellbeing, with the result that they were drawn to the work of the Brotherhood as by natural desire, and it was greatly extended. Among the initiates were farmers, traders, builders, teachers, soldiers, all working on the outer plane for material gain, yet moved by a spiritual urge. Scribes, musicians, dancers, officiants, servers or priests, also sought admission; and from among all these many were found fit after due testing and training to participate in the work.

Of course it was not all plain sailing. Ra-Hotep made a number of enemies in court circles and outside, particularly among those whose business was rapaciousness. At first many men and women sneered, and said it was impossible to eradicate people's deep-rooted selfishness. It was argued that this was a self-protective instinct and that men and women were meant to fight for themselves like the beasts. But despite all this, large numbers of the people responded, and they found that in practice it led them to happiness and true wealth, spiritual and material.

On one occasion, Ra-min-ati's trained gift of seership warned her that waves of envy and ill-will were being directed towards Ra-Hotep himself as well as his work, and she was shown in a dream that much of this originated with a chief overseer of works. At the first opportunity she asked Ra-Hotep if he was satisfied with his reports on Menepheti's treatment of his men. 'Yes', he replied. 'There seems no cause for complaint in that direction.'

'Well, I dreamt that Menepheti was scheming against you. I think there may be trouble among the men who are working on the new brotherhood temple.'

Ra-min-ati watched her husband who was leaning back in his chair, deep in thought. Ra-Hotep never failed to recognize and respect the methods of those who sometimes gave advice or warning through Ra-min-ati's lips. He knew that he might be used when they wished to engage with disintegrating forces such as could hinder and in time destroy the work of the White Lodge.

In fact it was no long time before discontent, slackness and indiscipline became rife among his men. Disheartened, unhappy, for he found it hard to understand why men who at one time had been contented should become dissatisfied and quarrelsome without obvious cause, he consulted Is-ra. 'I'm puzzled,' he said. 'There seems no reason why these men should behave like this, and the sad thing is that I can't see the remedy.'

'Brothers of the black magic', responded Is-ra, 'are cunning and subtle. They cover up their proceedings: even their victims are unaware of the way they are being used. Many an ugly deed is done innocently…. I mean that good and kind people who would abhor what is cruel and deceitful can be enslaved, unwilling and unknowing, by Brothers of the Shadow'.

'How can this be?', Ra-Hotep asked.

'In everyone, there are weaknesses that derive from the lower self, dark shades of character that can be exploited. It is on these that the workers of the black lodge concentrate, trying to irritate and inflame them. However innocent the victim is to begin with, by following the path that is so subtly suggested, one can quickly become their unconscious instrument.'

'I have never associated ordinary people with black magic. It is terrible to think that they can be influenced and corrupted in this way.'

'You have yet to learn that our world has languished in the grip of these dark masters for long periods of its history.'

'Then one would think that the world would have been completely destroyed by now!'

'It is not so', said Is-ra, 'because brothers and sisters of the white magic are vigilant and work without ceasing to preserve a balance between the constructive and the destructive'.

'I suppose there must be purpose in the activities of the dark brothers and sisters?'

'Yes indeed. Both purpose and plan. They too help to keep the balance. You find it difficult to understand this? Let it suffice when I tell you that black and white magic are really the same thing, the only difference in practice being that white magic is power used by absolute selflessness, while black magic is power used by absolute selfishness. This causes accumulations of what is called good and evil, both of which arise through personal choice, whether to ally one's self with the white magic or the black. If love of power governs a person, he or she will commit sins of cruelty, lust and violence. It is likely that Menepheti is not in himself what can be called a bad man, but he has grown jealous of you and your work. Because of this, he attracts the attention of brothers of the black magic—who see in him a useful instrument for their work of disintegration. Through him their power is amplified and through him they direct it to the workmen under his charge.'

'What do you suggest to counteract Menepheti's action?', Ra-Hotep asked, after a thoughtful silence.

'The only antidote to evil is good. The way to counteract hate is to practise its opposite. Observe and accept the action of opposites. You believe you are demonstrating the law of brotherhood through the work in your lodge? Put this principle into practice in the minutest particular in every human relationship and its magic will be seen.'

'You mean I'm to be as gentle with my enemy as he has been ruthless with me? And act in this spirit with the men who work under him?'

'It is the only answer.'

*

Menepheti lived in a house on the riverbank, like many government officials. He and his family had often exchanged hospitality with Ra-min-ati, and it was surprising that he should become antagonistic. But notwithstanding the awkwardness of the situation, Ra-min-ati was more and more impressed with the idea that she herself must talk things out with him.

Sitting one day by the lotus pond, looking across a lawn that sloped to the riverbank, she saw that an official barge was tying up at the landing stage. 'It looks like Menepheti's', she thought. 'He must be coming in response to my wish.' She went forward to greet him, perhaps not quite with the same spontaneity as on earlier occasions, but smiling. Try as she would she could not wholly overcome a sense of disappointment and hurt, but after some desultory conversation she summoned her strength and tried to dismiss all but kindness from her heart. 'I feel you are not altogether in sympathy with the principles embodied in Ra-Hotep's administration', she said.

Menepheti showed astonishment at the challenge, and no doubt he was shocked to discover that Ra-min-ati had known of his resentments. Appointed by high authority to direct the building of the new brotherhood lodge, he dared not question his instructions, although he revolted with all his being against having to build a house for an organisation of which he strongly disapproved. But he had spoken to no one about it and he was the more disturbed to find that Ra-min-ati was aware of his disloyalty, not only to herself and her husband but to the brotherhood. Now that the issue between them was definite he was glad to speak openly. 'It is true, Ra-min-ati', he said. 'I confess that I have been uneasy for the past year. I think my friends are foolish to pursue an ideal that I myself believe impractical and one that can bring little but disaster to the Egyptian people. What you have in view, Ra-min-ati, may have been all right in the beginning of time when men and women were almost slaves of the gods, and believed without question what we who are more civilized know to be mere superstition. We have travelled a long way since then. We Egyptians are practical people of affairs who see the folly of trying to put outworn ideas into practice. I tell you they can't work. This foolishness, if it becomes widely spread among the people, won't pay. No, Ra-min-ati. I set my face against it.'

He paused. 'I have asked myself several times', he went on,

'whether I should unburden myself to you or your husband, but I have been silent for the sake of our friendship. Now that you see what lies in my heart I can say without hesitation or equivocation that from now on I must do all in my power to prevent the work going forward'.

Although her dream had prepared her for this, Ra-min-ati felt distress. It was clear that the White Brothers were alert and watchful over those they guided. She would never have suspected Menepheti if they had not opened her eyes, and this in time to prevent serious harm. She felt a wave of sympathy for him, as she would have done for someone desperately ill. 'I am sorry', she said, 'that you think about it like this. I wish I could help. Do you wish to resign your appointment? What are your plans?'.

He shook his head. 'I fear I have come to the end. I have no plans. Wherever I look I can see nothing ... all is a blank to me'. He gazed with sad eyes across the desert; but though she talked to him, he did not waver in his intention to frustrate the building of the lodge if it lay in his power. He was subject to an overmastering impulse he did not understand.

Ra-min-ati fell silent, content to resign herself and her problem to the care of the gods. She knew that none had power to arrest Ra's will, though human kind might delay its manifestation. 'Can't you help me?', Menepheti pleaded at last. 'I came today almost against my will. A call reached me and I obeyed. Do you know what this means?'

'It means that willingly or unwillingly you are in Ra's power and he is directing you.'

They talked together for a little while longer and then Menepheti took leave. An indescribable pathos seemed to shadow him as his craft faded into the evening light; yet in a sense he went away a happier man, for his heart had been opened and confession made to those he designed to injure. In return, he received human understanding and sympathy.

Ra-min-ati remained musing and meditating in the solitude and peace of her garden a long time. There was much she did not understand, but she knew that love can solve every human problem. Together, Is-ra, Ra-Hotep and herself had caused light to flow into Menepheti's heart and begin the cleansing of dark places even against the will of his lower self.

A few days after this conversation a runner came to the house asking for her. He begged her to come with him to Menepheti, who lay dying. She left at once. She found that gloom had already fallen on the household, mourners were weeping in the outer courts and priests were in attendance at Menepheti's bedside. When she entered the room all others withdrew. Her friend, now but partially conscious, rallied when she grasped his hands, calling him by name. He greeted and thanked her in low, broken tones, saying, 'Dear Ra-min-ati, I slept a deep sleep and obtained understanding. Ra has revealed the future to me. I have seen for myself the magnitude of the task you and Ra-Hotep have begun. As I leave this world I am comforted by the assurance that I shall have other opportunities of helping you.'

After a long pause, and speaking with difficulty, he continued. 'My soul, as it passes from the body, makes this vow. When we meet again I will, if it pleases almighty Ra, surrender everything, my pride of office, my boasted intellect, to be your humble follower on the path, which alone, as now I know, leads to happiness and peace. I pledge myself to come to you, Ra-min-ati, as soon as the gods permit, and work faithfully with you to restore to the people the wisdom and truth of the White Light.'

Chapter 19

The Osiris Initiation

AFTER Menepheti's passing, all went well with the building of the temple. The workmen became friendly and co-operative. Perhaps Menepheti, from the beyond, was infusing them with his new spirit of goodwill and had put the work of redemption in hand. There were no more delays, and this was fortunate, as Pharaoh was growing old and the end of his time on earth seemed to be drawing near.

It was customary for the reigning Pharaoh to name his successor. As he had no daughter, he must name as successor one who had married a wife born in the royal line, in conformity with a law, which had obtained since the people of Atlantis came to Egypt. Ra-min-ati, his sister's daughter, had long been regarded as heir, and it was expected that she and her husband would jointly inherit the throne. Thus, when the time came these two were summoned to Pharaoh's presence, Is-ra being in attendance. Ra-Hotep was reminded of that audience, now twenty years ago, when he had been appointed administrator. Now he faced even greater responsibilities; but with Ra-min-ati beside him he would go forward with courage, thankful for the honour that was to be his.

As if in answer to his thoughts Pharaoh said, 'You have spent many years, Ra-Hotep, in service to your country. I have watched with growing respect. I have seen affection and trust spring up in the hearts of my people and you have always been loyal to me. Now Ra puts it into my heart to name you, with Ra-min-ati, as my successor. My time on earth is, for the present, drawing to a close. Soon I shall place the double crown on your head and put the symbols of power in your hands. I shall do this in peace. Your initiation will take place when the moon is full, in the temple of the Star beneath the Pyramid, where alone the highest degree of our Order is conferred. Meanwhile, meditate and pray, Ra-Hotep my son and Ra-min-ati my daughter.'

*

Their initiation was to take place at the ninth hour of the day of the full moon. They were to fast for twenty-four hours before the ceremony. This they did in the temple precinct, meditating in a garden so devised as to resemble a mountain rock-garden, full of rare blooms, patches of colour between which water cascaded down the rocks like falling jewels. A seat in a niche to one side of the waterfall commanded wide views of the Nile and they sat here, gazing across the river to fields where peasants were sowing corn.

Now Is-ra approached them. In spite of advancing years, his carriage was upright and his serene face bore no trace of strain or anxiety; indeed, there radiated from him an aura almost visible to the physical eyes. He greeted them. 'Do you remember, Ra-min-ati, when you first came to the temple? We found our way to a garden-sanctuary and spent many hours there learning to look through the veil of matter into the spirit world. You were curious about a door set in the wall, and I said that when the time came I would touch a spring and the door would open and you would pass through. The time has come. I will meet you both there at the ninth hour.' He left them to their thoughts.

*

They awaited him at the appointed time, clothed in robes of white linen, their only ornament the jewel each received when they were accepted into the service of the White Brotherhood.

It was a long time since Ra-min-ati had visited this garden-sanctuary, scene of her first initiation. Seeing the couch, she recalled the wonder of those early revelations, she remembered how Is-ra taught her to leave her sleeping body and rise to higher worlds. What mystery lay beyond the stone door?

Is-ra came in, blessed them and signing them to follow him touched a hidden spring. The stone door slid back and they stepped into a passage. The door closed behind them.

Now they were going down a stairway in soft light that came from the rock either side of it, and as they went farther into the labyrinths a yet more mysterious light illumined their way. It bathed walls that had gold veins in them like the pattern of trees stripped in winter. They went deeper and deeper. 'This will put you in mind', Is-ra said, 'of the spirit's descent into matter.' Then suddenly they came to the end of the passage and there was a stone door like the one they had entered above. Two priests, robed in blue, awaited them, and with no word spoken blindfolded the candidates, who heard a door slide and Is-ra's voice give a password. 'I stand surety for my companions', he added. The priests led them into the Hall of the Sphinx and acted as their guides and protectors throughout the ceremony.

They were dimly aware of a light, in stillness that was only broken by the sound of music as from a harp in the distance. Then a voice right in front of them said, 'Your destiny has brought you to the Hall of the Sphinx. Here is to be found the answer to the riddle of the universe, to solve which is the purpose of humananity's existence. Each person is composed of the four elements, earth, air, fire and water: your task is to discipline and control them. When each has gained self-knowledge and self-mastery each is ready for the degree that is conferred in this Hall. Thereafter the lower self has no value. Are you both ready to surrender all you have?'

Each of them said, 'I am'.

'Are you ready to look on the splendour of Ra's handi-work?'

'I am.'

'Then will you divest yourselves of all base metals that are components of human nature?'

'This I will do.'

'Will you suffer all that is base to be consumed in the fires of spirit and transmuted into the pure essence of the cosmos?'

'This I will do.'

'Then look on the glory of Ra's work.'

The bandages were taken from their eyes, and they saw they were standing before an altar in the shape of a double cube in blue stone that radiated light. They were in a temple on whose walls designs showing the stages of humanity's evolution were carved and painted. Four massive columns supported a roof on which scenes of angelic life were depicted; and the wall facing them was the head and front of a Sphinx in pure gold. They gazed at it, fascinated by the implications of this enigmatic symbol.

Now the guides led them seven times round the Hall and brought them again to the altar. The high priest made the sign of the double triangle that forms a six-pointed star. Then a door opened between the Sphinx's paws and they were led to the Hall of the Star beneath the pyramid, a blazing hall in the form of a six-pointed star, so that they seemed to stand within a solid jewel, a perfect crystal, suspended in space, beyond the limitations of their three-dimensional world, for now they had entered a higher state of being. A priest stood at each point of the star, at its centre the Hierophant before whom they were to prostrate themselves in token of surrender to the Supreme.

The Hierophant broke silence. 'This is the highest peak in the range your souls have climbed. Now you find yourselves within the compass of the perfect star, the primordial symbol of life on earth through which the cosmos manifests. Emblem of the cosmos itself, it will be found in the lowest manifestation of the Creator, the minutest particle of dust. It is in the shape of the simplest flower, and in the perfected soul.

'The symbol of human beings on earth is the pentagram, or five-pointed star, but in the six-pointed star we see the completed union of two triangles, unification of the two aspects of human life. The upward-pointing triangle is the physical aspect, the downward-pointing one is the descent of spirit. The two interpenetrating signify human nature in balance between heaven and earth. This symbol speaks also of the blending of opposites, good and evil, light and darkness, self and selflessness.

'Here in this chamber alone can there be contact with the Star Circle in heaven, the circle in which dwell those made perfect through the Redeemer, who from time immemorial has descended into the darkness of this planet to teach humanity the secret of the heavenly life. Children of earth, may you see the glory of the life prepared for you from the beginning.'

The candidates felt themselves being raised. They were no longer conscious as man and woman but as souls in the

*The hierophant was the interpeter of the Ancient Mysteries.

realm of souls, in the company of spirit beings who shone with pure radiance. The chamber too shone with resplendent light from an invisible sun, in whose heart the star-jewel hung. They were in the jewel and looked out with magic vision on a world made perfect, where people lived in harmony, health and contentment.

The Hierophant spoke again. 'We show you Ra's will for the sons and daughters of earth. We show you human kind's destiny, the end to which creation labours through the efforts of all humanity men and women. But this lies within one's own will, for it is in this that rests the power to accept or reject the will of the Creator, to refuse it or to possess it.'

When he ceased, Ra-min-ati and Ra-Hotep looked into a face, which although it was a man's was also the visage of truth, love and peace, and their hearts were filled with goodwill to human kind. Silence reigned, a silence of power and illumination; and now the King of Light stood before them. It seemed the temple was built of celestial substance; the columns, lit of themselves, threw a soft, rosy glow over the assembly. The walls, veined with soft colours, were translucent. Strains of music stole on the scene: it might have been angels that sang praise and glory. Ra-min-ati and Ra-Hotep were in an illimitable time and space, lifted to still greater heights, for the ritual had released them and they had travelled in astral consciousness to heaven. In place of the Hierophant the Grand Master stood; he spoke and all heaven seemed to vibrate with the music.

'My children say Osiris was slain. They say his body was dismembered and enclosed in a box of base metal, cast into the abyss, utterly destroyed. They say Isis gathered the fragments and remade him, and they begat Horus, the perfect human being. Let this put you continually in mind that the indestructible cannot be destroyed. Evil can never slay the perfect form of the Son of Ra or annihilate the divine spirit. It rises again and again and returns to its like on earth, and thus it will be until all people, even the lowliest, are raised into itself.

'Return to your place and rule over Ra's children. Guide them by true vision of the all-seeing eye, the light that is in you. Serve them with unflinching devotion, ever mindful of the responsibility now laid on you to provide for their physical, mental and spiritual needs according to your resources. Do not let the memory of this moment fade from your hearts. Give me your word. Do you solemnly pledge yourselves to be true and loyal servants of the Grand Company henceforth?'

'We do so pledge ourselves.'

'Do you promise to serve all others with the strength of your body, providing them with means to acquire the needs of bodily life for themselves?'

'We do so promise.'

'Do you solemnly swear to give of yourselves in all forms of mental and spiritual culture, so that your people lack nothing for the pursuit of knowledge in the ancient arts and sciences?'

'We do solemnly swear it.'

'Are you ready to renounce worldly power, honour and possessions, to be nothing in the eyes of others, if this be the will of the triune One?'

'We are ready to surrender all things if it be the will of the triune One.'

'Then rise.' Hands lifted them. The power of the Triune One permeated body, soul and spirit. They rested a long time in communion with heaven.

*

When they returned to earth-consciousness, they were lying in a sarcophagus. They had no idea how long they had been there, but it felt as if after passing through death into a glorious state they had returned into bodies that were heavy, cold and encased as are the dead. After many hours a priest came, helped them to rise and led them back to the Hall of the Sphinx, where they stood once more before the Hierophant.

'A task of heaviest responsibility lies before you', he said. 'You cannot hope to fulfil your vows of your own strength. Therefore we in this Brotherhood remind you that Ra is ever merciful and remembers the need of those who serve him in the dark world. He will send brothers and sisters of the White Light to your aid. They will be your never-failing companions while you hold office. Earth people are frail and cannot be depended upon to maintain the necessary standard of accomplishment, for their flesh weakens them; but their friends of the spirit will not fail them in whatever need. I commend you, then, to their love and care. Look to them as they look to almighty Ra and you will walk in peace all your days on earth.'

Chapter 20

Coronation

THE ROYAL city was alive again with people singing and dancing, for the joint-Pharaoh was to be crowned in the Temple of Ra and driven to the palace for enthronement. Crowds lined the route; still greater numbers collected outside the temple and before the palace. The people amused themselves with music, flower-throwing and banner-waving while they awaited their new rulers.

A distinguished company gathered in the temple. Music of flute and harp grew to a climax as trumpeters announced the arrival of the heirs to the throne. Entering, they moved slowly to their places on golden thrones raised high northeast of the altar. At the same time, aged Pharaoh was conducted to his throne on the northwest side. A moment later, he came down to the foot of the seven broad steps and the music faded. The heirs came down too and faced him.

Is-ra, wearing the insignia of his office, called on the assembly to witness that Pharaoh was present for the last time, for it was his will that the government of his people should pass to younger hands. 'Before you', Is-ra continued, 'stand Ra-min-ati and her consort Ra-Hotep, who are known to you as wise, true counsellors of the Royal House. They come having been duly prepared and initiated into the higher mysteries of almighty Ra. It only remains then for them to be presented to you, their people, as the anointed representatives of the most holy light.

Faithful subjects of the Two Lands, we proclaim that Ra-min-ati and Ra-Hotep are henceforth royal Pharaoh.'

White-robed priests chanted in unison on behalf of the people, 'We proclaim. We welcome. We acknowledge them as Pharaoh.'

The two were conducted to the throne on which the abdicating Pharaoh was now seated. Each in turn took his hand in both of theirs and raised it to lips and forehead in token of affection and loyalty. He then lifted his hand in blessing and laid it on his heart.

Next Ra-min-ati and Ra-Hotep were led to kneeling-stools before the golden altar ablaze with lamps. As they knelt, the high priest took crook and flail from cushions held out to him by two priests and put them in the new rulers' hands. Then he placed on the head of each a golden crown or circlet on whose front the figure of a bird was mounted. The two rose and faced the assembly. Music burst forth while they went hand-in-hand to their chariot. In sunlight pouring from a blue sky they were driven to the palace by a broad avenue flanked with sphinxes. They mounted the palace steps to sounds of cheering and singing and turned to acknowledge the acclamation. Then they passed into the palace and the gates closed.

THE END OF THE STORY

White Eagle's Work in the Present Day

WHITE Eagle is still at work spreading the 'white carpet' over earth. In the year 1936, he and an invisible company directed me to organise a group of men and women willing to practise brotherhood among themselves and ready to be channels through which light can be sent to the minds of men and women throughout the world, and especially to those with responsibility and authority. Before the Second World War broke out, messages were received from him concerning the importance of this work during the 'Years of Fire', in view of the possibility that greed and passion might destroy humanity. We thought these messages referred to the War, but we have learnt that the 'Years of Fire' are the years of transition from the Age of Pisces and orthodox Christianity to the Age of Aquarius and brotherhood, the Golden Age.

The group is trained to receive power from an invisible source, and in unison to project good thought or light into the ether, which when correctly, powerfully and persistently directed can in the end produce a significant effect on individual and collective minds. Needless to say, the work is impersonal, selfless, without ambition, having no political bias, and undertaken only with the aim of awakening the light that is hidden in every human heart.

Speaking to the group, White Eagle said: You are contributing to humanity a substance, which will be constructive and helpful in the years to come. You are sending into the finer ethers vibrations of light and sound that will find their mark: sooner or later the human recipient will respond. This is what we are all striving for, although we who are discarnate are better able to see the effect of your collective thought. Time and space are no barriers. What lies in the invisible and is hidden in silence today will be visible and audible in humanity's life tomorrow.

'The Brotherhood is founded on the principle of simple, loving service, absolute selflessness. Many believe that a man or woman can best serve in isolation; but we have learnt that the individual must work in collaboration in order if he or she wishes to forward the process of spiritual evolution. The real cause of all chaos is separateness. There can be no such thing as splendid isolation—all are interdependent. It is a grave as well as an uplifting thought that no-one can live to him- or herself. The one who indulges in destructive, negative, critical thought, injures first self, then others.

'Be a light-bearer. In Egypt the candidate for initiation had only to remember that the light within would protect him or her. It would at once carry each one through deep waters and raging fires, and rescue each from the serpents on the path. So will the light sustain you in the days to come. But you do not work for yourselves. If a group of brother–sisters in the light of Christ work together in courage and serenity, humanity may be saved. We give you this charge.'

The following words of White Eagle's will serve to make clearer what is done.

'It would be well for the brethren to picture to themselves what happens on the inner planes when they meet. The invisible brethren prepare for an hour or longer before the meeting to concentrate the power and light, so that those who enter the lodge step, as it were, out of earthly darkness into the light, and the process of the lifting of the consciousness begins from that moment. The emotional, mental and intuitive life of each brother and sister is unified, because as you aspire to the Great

White Spirit so your consciousness is raised and all function as one, on the inner planes.

'On the inner planes, thought is like a flash of light, instantaneous. On the outer plane, when a voice calls, the physical hearing responds. Call with your thought and the mind-life will answer. Call from within your soul and there will be a soul reply. Project light to another; light is generated by Brothers–Sisters in the invisible world who can transmit it through you, if you are selfless; project light to another soul and the soul will receive it. It will respond to the soul-light. The power will illuminate the soul and gradually permeate the physical body and outward life. Use this power to heal the sick. You may be in time to heal the body, to cleanse it of the poison accumulated by wrong thoughts, wrong emotions and errors manifold. In any case, you will be in time to enlighten, help and strengthen the soul. No selfless effort is ever wasted.'

It was in this way that Brotherhoods worked in Atlantis, the Andes, Egypt, and Europe. We have reached the Aquarian Age, whose symbol is a man carrying a pitcher of water, the water of life, spirit. This symbol recalls the words of Christ, when he bade his disciples go before him into the city of Jerusalem and there prepare for the feast of communion or the feast of remembrance. The disciples, you will note, were to precede him to the holy city of Jerusalem and were to follow 'the man bearing the pitcher of water'. This man would lead them to the 'upper room', where they were to make ready for the feast of remembrance—the holy communion. The 'upper room' signifies the higher-mind or higher-consciousness of human kind, that which lies above the level of materialism, signified by 'the inn' of which the 'upper room' formed a part.

The Age of Aquarius into which humanity has entered

is that New Age of the Brotherhood. Those who guide and inspire the human race, under the law of the Christ Spirit, are at present principally concerned with the establishing on earth of the spirit of true brotherhood and goodwill—the city of light, the holy city described in the Revelation of St John.

The Vision of the Plumed Serpent

It is told in Part I how a Mayan-Indian girl, Minesta, was sent for with her father and brother by a Master of the White Light and how, in a temple among pines on some height in the Andes, they saw in what manner the white light was used in the long past, as it is used now and will be used in the future, to heal, illumine and inspire human kind.

'Plumed Serpent' was the name given by the Sages of the Ancient Wisdom to those initiated into the mysteries and reborn with the fuller consciousness to which all souls will evolve.

A Plumed Serpent, then, is a fully-evolved being, an 'Illumined One', a son–daughter of God, one who has established this son- or daughtership by long and arduous labour; one in whom the spiritual creative power has risen from the roots of the Tree of Life, the generative organs, and ascended the spinal column to the crown of the head, where it flowers. A Plumed Serpent is one in whom the creative power, transmuting the animal instincts, has reached the highest stage of consciousness, illumination, and become the Word itself. Those whose inner eye is open can see the light from such a one radiating like an aura, a headdress of soft, white plumes.

The experience I had in the Andes, the glimpse of a

Plumed Serpent, has been repeated in this life. Once, in sleep, in vision too vivid to be mere fanciful dream, I was taken once more to a mountain on which stood a temple, open at the sides, with domed roof supported by columns, whose stones radiated soft light of many colours. The roof was a glowing canopy. I entered and found myself in an assembly of White Brothers who knelt in prayer for those far away on the plain below, those on earth. I saw a white dove come down into the midst of the kneeling group. As I stood I became aware of a presence at my side, and across the lapse of centuries I recognized the gentle and gracious presence of the Master and Teacher to whom I had once before been summoned. Standing apart, I watched with awe while yet more white-robed brothers and sisters gathered. Slowly, with perfect poise and dignity, they came into the circular temple to the throb of music that rose presently in a crescendo of powerful chords and then died into profound stillness.

Still they entered between two massive columns, which formed the entrance to the temple. I noticed that each robed figure seemed to emit a soft radiance, especially round the head, a sight that reminded me of paintings showing the haloed head of disciple or Master. The aura was definite and unmistakable. I began to remember words spoken by one I loved long ago with love almost amounting to worship: 'Look for those who are to come, who will be known as Plumed Serpents'.

What had been a mystery became clear. I was seeing these souls in process of transmutation, of illumination. At last, they came to rest before the central altar, each with right hand on the heart. The noble figure of their leader, crowned with a head-dress of great white plumes, moved forward and lifted from the altar a blazing star, the symbol of this brotherhood. He spoke, in words that sounded in my heart like chords of music.

'God's will is that you love … all people. That you constantly send out goodwill, light … to all humanity. We are to work, unknown, on human minds and hearts. The years speed by. Humanity has passed the darkest stages of its journey and is awakening to the light that is Christ, perfect son of God, perfected son of human kind. As you overcome your desires and passions, your lower, animal self, you make room for the great Brother that is Christ to manifest in your life. This growth is your sacred heritage. Progress in spiritual evolution is your destiny. What you begin today you will continue tomorrow; and in the afterlife you will still work to guide, inspire and bless human kind.'

The words died away and the music faded. Wondering, I watched the white-robed group grow into a vast company. The altar in their midst was afire, and in its centre there glowed a rose light, the colour of the Grail. I watched while the Master, the Plumed Serpent, encircled by the great white company, blessed all humanity; then all merged into that one Figure, a being become godlike, the Plumed Being of grace and wisdom, one of the 'Illumined Ones'.

I looked again and saw only the White Light blazing out of heaven. I turned my face earthward and went back to the plains, where human beings toil and grieve and begin the long journey home.